D0076631

Toward Ritual Transformation

Toward Ritual Transformation

Remembering Robert W. Hovda

Gabe Huck

Robert W. Hovda

Virgil C. Funk

J. Michael Joncas

Nathan D. Mitchell

James Savage

John Foley, S.J.

A PUEBLO BOOK

The Liturgical Press   Collegeville Minnesota

www.litpress.org

A Pueblo Book published by The Liturgical Press

Design by Frank Kacmarcik, Obl.S.B. Photo courtesy of the National Association of Pastoral Musicians.

© 2003 by The Order of Saint Benedict, Collegeville, Minnesota. All rights reserved. No part of this book may be reproduced in any form or by any means, electronic or mechanical, including photocopying, recording, taping, or any retrieval system, without the written permission of The Liturgical Press, Collegeville, Minnesota 56321. Printed in the United States of America.

1   2   3   4   5   6   7   8

Library of Congress Cataloging-in-Publication Data

Toward ritual transformation : remembering Robert W. Hovda /
    Gabe Huck ... [et al.].
        p. cm.
    Includes bibliographical references.
    ISBN 0-8146-6196-3 (alk. paper)
        1. Catholic Church—Liturgy. I. Hovda, Robert W. II. Huck, Gabe.
BX1970 .T66 2003
264'.02—dc21   2002035912

Contents

Foreword

Transformation and Hovda belong together.

"Musical Liturgy Transforms" was the theme of the Twenty-fifth Anniversary Convention of the National Association of Pastoral Musicians (NPM), a membership organization dedicated to fostering the art of musical liturgy. "Musical Liturgy is normative" was the theme of the first convention, and twenty-five years later, we realized that musical liturgy is transformative, and, indeed, had itself been transformed.

Five of the essays in this book were originally presented as The Hovda Lectures and given at that twenty-fifth anniversary convention. The Hovda Lecture Series continues and is designed to provide a more reflective approach to musical liturgy, challenging the participants and the readers to a more serious reflection on the role of Church music in the Roman Catholic Liturgy. The theme of "transformation" was tied in with the overall theme of the National NPM Convention—but stands alone as a wonderful opportunity for pastoral practioner, student of the liturgy, or pastoral musician to sail a little deeper into the sea of liturgical study.

The Hovda Lectures were named, appropriately, after one of the leading liturgists of the post-Vatican II era, a priest who preached transformation all his life. It is only fitting that the two themes—Hovda's life and transformation—are woven together in this book. Gabe Huck, a lifelong friend of Hovda's, sums up his life so well that the reader who is unfamiliar with Bob's life will feel its power, and those of us who had the privilege to know him can hear again his rasping voice calling us to transformation through Gabe's words. But if that is not enough, we have added a talk that Hovda gave at the 1982 Convention of NPM. Read it again! His words are as alive and challenging today on these printed pages as they were when he first gave it twenty years ago. Amazingly, some truths are always transformative. Transformation and Hovda belong together.

We are grateful for The Liturgical Press, especially Mark Twomey and Colleen Stiller, who make this publication possible. We are forever grateful for Dr. Gordon Truitt, who serves as general editor of NPM, and who edited this project with the help of Virginia Sloyan, longtime friend of Bob Hovda. We are especially grateful for Dr. J. Michael McMahon, president and CEO of NPM, who guided this work to publication.

"A believer knows that the faith community—the Church—is never finalized or finished, never an accomplished fact but always a pilgrimage, seeking, growing and helping the world grow toward what Scripture calls the reign of God." Our hope is that this first collection of Hovda Lectures is a step *"Toward Ritual Transformation."*

Virgil C. Funk
December 8, 2002

A Tree Planted by a Stream

Gabe Huck

You already know Robert Hovda. If you work at making liturgy the strong and sturdy and beautiful work of the assembly, you know him through what is perhaps the most amazing document to come from an office of the United States Conference of Catholic Bishops—*Environment and Art in Catholic Worship*. Hovda was the principal author. Even if you were still very young when he died in February 1992, you know him in the generation of present leaders who found in him an authentic voice persistently articulating the liturgical reform as essential to the larger reforming of our Church and our world. And if you have the good fortune to have been present at some gatherings when he spoke, then you know him well: the sharp humor, the raspy whisper of a voice, the well-built sentences, and the passion that informed all else.

When Hovda died in a New York City project apartment (a Lower East Side building from the New Deal era with, to be kind, aging plumbing), his library filled only a dozen short shelves. One four-drawer file cabinet was sufficient for hundreds of folders filled with carbon copies (he never made it to the word-processing age) from decades of letters, lectures, books, and articles. The art he had collected over many years—folk art mostly and especially pottery—took up a little more space. His body went to a medical school.

In his last years, Bob Hovda was happily retired, scraping by on a tiny pension and some writing and speaking income: a budget that seldom included new clothes but gave priority to theater and opera tickets (he liked a good seat and being early and he was generous with his "bravos" if a performance pleased him). He hadn't owned a car in years—to the great relief of his friends—but he knew the city's subways with precision. Saturday nights he waited impatiently at the corner for the Sunday *Times* to be delivered before he'd go home. He had stopped drinking in the 1970s after years of struggle and much failure, and he took his AA responsibilities seriously even in retirement. Cigarettes and coffee were other matters, however.

When considering the city, the world, and the Church, as he often did even if he would profess to have given up on all of them, Hovda had about him more than a little of the curmudgeon in the second meaning of the word: one who hates hypocrisy and pretense and has the temerity to say so, one with the habit of pointing out unpleasant facts in an engaging and humorous manner. By the same token, he gave his trust and friendship to those he perceived as fairly low in hypocrisy and pretense. At his death he was in lively contact with friends he'd known for fifty years and friends from every decade since, a group of women and men diverse by almost any measure. Some of them were drawn to him because of the wisdom he brought to the liturgical renewal, but many barely knew what he'd done for a living.

Robert Walker Hovda was born in 1920 in Wisconsin, but the family soon crossed the river into Minnesota. A brother was born just as the Great Depression was beginning, and the family knew unemployment and hardship. Though his earliest religious formation was in the Lutheran Church, as a teenager Hovda found companions, the social gospel, and a lifetime's direction in the Methodist youth movement. He went to listen to speakers like Bayard Rustin and Norman Thomas, was editor of the school paper at Central High School in Minneapolis, and joined the Socialist Party before graduation. At Hamline University Hovda joined the Episcopal Church (but took with him the strong social gospel he had found in the Methodist Church) and continued reading authors who brought together his concerns for justice, pacifism, economic reform, and worship. He worked nights until the family needed more help, then left college to work in a Ford plant. It was 1941.

A few months before Pearl Harbor, the twenty-one-year-old Hovda wrote to a pastor in St. Paul:

"We believe that those who cannot conscientiously return evil for evil, reviling for reviling, who cannot see the salvation of democracy in its abandoning, who believe the way of war to be thoroughly destructive not only to men's bodies, but also to their spiritual capacities should, as well as the conscientious militarist, have the opportunity of following the will of God as they know it."

Less than a year later all the reading and discussion came to the test: Hovda was drafted and applied for status as a conscientious objector. It is difficult for us today to imagine what a lonely stance that was for someone not a member of the so-called "peace churches." Many who applied were refused and chose prison rather than military service. Others accepted non-combatant work in the military. The form of application for conscientious objector status contained this question: "Explain how, when, and from whom or from what source you received the training and acquired the belief which is the basis of your claim." Hovda replied:

"I am a Christian because I have been brought up in the fellowship of the Church and of other Christians, because I believe that the Christian Church stands for Truth and Reality in the midst of a largely false and unrealistic world, because my total experience seems to confirm the truth of the Catholic Faith. I believe an intelligent criticism of this faith will find the law of Love at its heart (e.g., the commands to overcome evil with good, to return good for evil, to turn the other cheek, to love our neighbors as ourselves, to love our enemies, etc.). The Catholic faith implies a confidence in the power of good will, of friendliness, of love to accomplish that which violence can not. The writings and lives of the Saints and of those in all generations who seem to most resemble Jesus make clear to me the incongruity of attempting to achieve good ends by evil means. I can assign no particular date to this realization that the power of love is stronger than that of the sword and that, for Christians, its practice is a moral imperative. My belief is the natural result of a growth in Christian faith."

To a question about how his behaviors demonstrated his beliefs, he answered in part: "Since I first talked before youth groups I have consistently advocated the abrogating of the war method by Christians and obedience to the plain counsels of our Lord. I have attempted in my own life, very imperfectly of course, to do the same."

The draft board voted three to one to grant Hovda conscientious objector status and he was sent to a Civilian Public Service Camp in New Hampshire where the daily work was removing trees blown down in a hurricane years before. He was there only three months, but that was enough to find companions who would be his friends for fifty years. This small camp had many Roman Catholics ("artists, eccentrics, totalitarians, etc.," Hovda later wrote); they were cared for there by the Catholic Worker Movement, which had itself lost much support in 1940 when Dorothy Day insisted on strict pacifism.

Hauling dead trees soon seemed pointless, and Hovda asked for hospital work. He was assigned to a Catholic hospital in Chicago. But the question of cooperation with the government and the military in any form was now growing stronger. By June 1943 Hovda and a few others were ready to refuse any cooperation with the draft system. They left their assigned jobs, were arrested, and were expecting to be sent to prison for at least three years.

His experiences with Catholics in New Hampshire and Chicago brought Hovda to a decision: While awaiting trial, he took instructions from a Carmelite priest and became a Roman Catholic on the night before his first court hearing. In the pre-war years Hovda had come close to entering an Episcopal seminary. Now he began immediately to look for a Roman Catholic seminary. The very long letter he sent "to whom it may concern" at dozens of seminaries may leave us unsurprised that they all turned him down. These excerpts from twenty-three-year-old Robert Hovda's seminary application reveal the thought and the literary abilities that would serve the Church for five decades:

"I have recently been received into the Roman Catholic Church as a convert and intend to pursue studies for the priesthood. I entered into a Civilian Public Service camp last fall acutely conscious of my opposition as a Christian to both war and conscription. My accent was on opposition to war, however, and I hoped to find in a Civilian Service for conscientious objectors opportunity not only to bear witness against war, but also to serve my fellows and become part of the movement towards true order in justice and peace. There is nothing basic in the situation I know now which I did not believe or fear then. I thought acquiescence in conscription for war would be a compromise to begin all compromises. I feared that the Civilian Public Service program would become just a niche for conscientious objectors in an increasingly fascist war conscription system, obscuring their importance and effect as a minority group . . . but I did not then realize, as clearly as I do now this fact: that modern conscription and modern war are one evil inextricably bound together . . .

"The trend toward fascism in government in this country is so obvious as to need little emphasis . . . . Regimentation of Japanese Americans into concentration camps, anti-strike legislation, and freezing of all wages and of workers in their jobs, impending conscription of women, the threat of permanent conscription, all of these are flagrant examples and tragic witnesses . . . .

"I believe I have a vocation to the Catholic priesthood and to turn aside from that goal to follow a war-making state—that would be apostasy and would rest as a sin upon my conscience. Absolutely fundamental in Catholic teaching is an insistence that free choice of one's state of life is necessary to the development of the person. The choice as the state put it before me today is clear: it is between voluntary submission to a conscription which takes me from where I rightfully belong and will to be, into a mechanistic structure filled with other coerced individuals on the one hand; and on the other, entrance into a particular state of life to which I believe I have a vocation. There is only one possible answer to that choice, whether the latter course involves suffering or not . . ."

When the trial came, the judge unexpectedly proposed that if Hovda could find a school that would admit him, he could begin studies during a period of probation. But all the seminaries who replied said no, thanks; some added that they already had more seminarians than the dioceses needed. One letter, however, suggested he apply to Saint John's in Collegeville, Minnesota. Hovda did and was accepted by that school as quickly as he had been rejected by all the others, even though he was without a bishop sponsoring him and without any means of support. (The other conscientious objectors who had walked away from the conscription system with him received prison time of three years or more.)

Hovda's movement from the Lutheran Church he attended as a child, to the Methodist activism of his teenage years, to the ritual patterns of Anglican and Roman Catholic Churches was not a movement of turning his back on earlier experiences but of a continuing formation that embraced those experiences. He brought to his Roman Catholicism and to Roman Catholics the breadth of that formation and an essential respect for other traditions. He recognized how the personal and public struggle for justice needs and draws strength from the full ritual life of a church, but he was under no illusions. Hovda was never the stereotype of the starry-eyed convert to Catholicism. His final religious home would not be spared a lifetime of criticism as sharp as it was loving.

When Hovda arrived at St. John's, the college and monastery had already been for some years a center of Catholic renewal. Virgil Michel had died in 1938, still a young man, but young patristics scholar Godfrey Diekmann and others carried on the work. Michel taught by word and extraordinary example that this renewal was not to be about liturgy alone but about Catholic life in the public arena and in the household. St. John's was one piece of a quilt of renewal slowly being assembled.

Hovda had already experienced the Catholic Worker Movement at the camp in New Hampshire. By the time he was completing his college years and beginning to study theology at St. John's, Catholics in cities and rural areas in various parts of the country were experimenting with a variety of movements—labor, student, young people, rural life, family—and through it all the formation of an involved and responsible Catholic laity. Participation in the liturgy went hand-in-hand with participation in the Church's mission. Since 1940 The Liturgical Conference had been offering annual Liturgical Weeks. These were Chautauqua-like events, popping up here and there across the country, at which those involved in aspects of this ecclesial renewal—Bible, liturgy, social justice, labor, rural life, catechetics—could rally and study and draw strength for an often lonely struggle back home.

Years after Hovda's arrival at Collegeville, Godfrey Diekmann wrote in a letter to Todd Dominique (whose master's thesis was most helpful in preparing this introduction) of the years when Diekmann was teaching and Hovda was studying at St. John's:

"While Bob had the passion for social justice before he came to St. John's, he learned here that the liturgy is the foundation and the constant source of commitment to social justice. The liturgy *demands* such a commitment . . . Bob eagerly picked it up and it became integral to his life's apostolate."

In 1949 Hovda finished his studies at St. John's. Along the way Bishop Muensch of Fargo had accepted him as a seminarian for that diocese. After ordination, Hovda served at the Fargo cathedral for five years and for five more in two rural parishes. Through speaking and through letters, articles, and book reviews in many Catholic publications, this man in far-off Fargo became familiar to those working in various aspects of the movement. He was increasingly in touch with artist Frank Kacmarcik and with Maurice Lavanoux, whose *Liturgical Arts* magazine was bringing to Americans the best work done around the world as well as at home. The quality of beauty in liturgy and the culture became for Hovda an essential part of the foundation for any ecclesial renewal.

But what was life like in the parish in the 1950s for one with such a background and such a vision? We can look through the window of two letters (with gratitude again to Todd Dominique for his work on the Hovda files). Here is Hovda in 1954 when Catholics had been so often found on the bandwagon of Senator Joseph McCarthy:

"This week I have again been beaten about the ears by my auxiliary bishop, in a half-hour interview concerning my imprudences generally and particularly . . . The occasion for this latest attack on my scant virtue was a private note I wrote to a Wisconsin newspaperman (he started the recall movement against McCarthy) congratulating him and thanking him. The damn fool put it in news releases that went all over the country. There it was—everywhere—in plain print that Fr. Robert Hovda of Fargo, North Dakota, didn't like Senator McCarthy.

"The fact that all the clergy who are mutes have been quoted in periodicals the length and breadth of the land in support of the Wisconsin demagogue apparently does not alter the fact that the mistake is mine. So I should shut up more, pray, and contemplate. I agree. But that wasn't his gripe. It wasn't even that he personally liked McCarthy. It was just that the whole concept of a priest who can think in terms of such a letter, in politico-social terms, who shows such an immoderate interest in a world whose only real business is the financing of ecclesiastical projects . . . such a concept separates the Bishop from his roots, leaves him stranded, fighting mad.

"So what the hell do we do . . . Apart from totally irrational obedience, there was about as much theological force or persuasion in what he said as there is in the content of the weekly *Register*. Nothing is safe, nothing is appreciated by mediocrity, purely glandular activity. If there is a spark, kill it; it may accidentally become a flame. If there is a stream of living water, stuff a rag into the hole; don't channel it [and] direct it to a parched land.

"Where do they drain the humanity out of potential hierarchs? Is there a special processing plant over there somewhere? And what kind of acid do they mix with the shit that takes its place?"

A few years later, when he was a pastor in rural North Dakota, he wrote of two very different experiences of the Church:

"This afternoon I attended with two of my parishioners a diocesan meeting, preliminary to a provincial prayer 'crusade.' It was one of those rare occasions when priests and lay representatives from our whole diocese meet together. We were told (with a moving sincerity and fervor) that 1) the best family prayer is the family rosary, 2) the family rosary will keep the family together, will cure all the ills of our day, will in large part eliminate the need for psychiatrists and social reformers, 3) we would do well to abandon 'theorizing,' programs, institutional reforms, to stop worrying about politics and economics and international affairs, because the only thing that does any good basically is the family rosary, 4) it is very important to follow the theory, or program or institution, outlined for the house to house family rosary drive, 5) the crusade works.

"Now let's face it. This is our problem in a capsule. Or pill. I was saved because I came home as promptly as possible and this evening celebrated the Eucharist together with a fragment of my parish. We gathered around the holy Table, we listened to the word of God, we presented ourselves, our lives, our work, our world, our friends and neighbors, our inadequacies too, at the altar with bread and wine, we offered the memorial sacrifice, we shared the holy Bread. And in this act we realized the Church, we built the Church, we lived as Church, and grew, and learned."

If we have taken much time with the first half of Hovda's life, it is because that is less well known and because it is so fascinating to see in his searching and his courage the directions that would guide him and bless all of us through the second half of his life. And that half can then be told more quickly.

Hovda left North Dakota in 1959 and returned for only one extended stay, 1963 to 1965 when he served in campus ministry. But he visited regularly, and the church of that diocese never forgot him but took his later work to heart and kept him in prayer.

In 1959 Gerard Sloyan, then chair of the Department of Religious Education at The Catholic University of America, invited Hovda to come and teach about liturgy and ecumenism. Sloyan was in the process of making that department into a major force for renewal in the American church just as the Council was getting underway. But neither in these years, nor in the late 1970s, when Hovda taught at the Jesuit School of Theology in Chicago, was he at home in the classroom. He was far more comfortable at the typewriter, in discussions, and in teaching liturgy by good example.

All of these became possible for him in 1965 when he began thirteen years as an editor with The Liturgical Conference. The Conference, in the years just before Vatican II, had for the first time been able to open an office. The annual Liturgical Weeks continued into the 1970s, but publishing became more and more the Conference's vehicle of teaching, and Hovda was in great part responsible for its success.

These were the years of optimism, the years when the Council's work was given initial practical shape by various groups of bishops and scholars, revising one by one the rites that had remained largely unchanged for four hundred years. They were years of doing what hadn't been done in anyone's memory: introducing Roman Catholics, including the clergy, not only to the vernacular in their liturgy but to orders of service that called for full, conscious, and active participation. Though people had little to go by in figuring out what that might mean, most embraced the reforms with good will. The ferment in the Roman Church was something of a catalyst: Anglicans, Lutherans, Methodists, Presbyterians, and others began their own process of liturgical renewal.

The Liturgical Conference, both in the annual gatherings and in its new publications, embraced ecumenism and tried in every publication to hold together the assembly that had come into being through the previous thirty years: Bible, justice, catechetics, liturgy. But now the Conference also had the role of a mentor in bringing congregations and their leaders into participatory liturgy. Hovda's influence was felt in all the directions taken by the Conference in these years.

Living Worship, a four-page, 8½ x 11 newsletter, became his monthly instruction to all who would listen. Many Roman Catholic dioceses made sure every priest received a copy. In these pages Hovda was at his best: taking some particular aspect of the liturgy and bringing to it a freshness that lacked nothing in scholarship, nothing in breadth. Whether he talked about music, the entrance rite, anointing, or the roles of various ministers in liturgy, the insights came from the whole breadth of his life and interest. Connections were made everywhere, and justice and the arts were integral to every discussion.

It is in the pages of *Living Worship* that Hovda worked out the ideas that would later become the document of the Bishops' Committee on the Liturgy, *Environment and Art in Catholic Worship*. Such documents are never attributed, and certainly Hovda's basic text was altered by committee work before its 1978 publication. But his hand is clear not only in its content but also in its welcome elegance. The document had a profound impact on new building and renovation, but it was far more: a passionate exposition of the vision made possible by the *Constitution on the Sacred Liturgy* of Vatican II. It was for some in the Catholic Church too much. Those who wanted to close off the reforms never accepted the authority of *Environment and Art in Catholic Worship*, and in 2000 it was officially replaced by a document utterly lacking in vision and poetry. But for those whose agenda remains the reform commanded by Vatican II, *Environment and Art in Catholic Worship* is a primary source of insight and inspiration. Nowhere until this document had the implications of the Council's teaching on participation been expounded so clearly in terms of the centrality of the assembly itself. A few paragraphs that are vintage Hovda:

"Christians have not hesitated to use every human art in their celebration of the saving work of God in Jesus Christ, although in every historical period they have been influenced, at times inhibited, by cultural circumstances. In the resurrection of the Lord, all things are made new. Wholeness and healthiness are restored, because the reign of sin and death is conquered. Human limits are still real and we must be conscious of them. But we must also praise God and give God thanks with the human means we have available. God does not need liturgy, people do, and people have only their own arts and styles of expression with which to celebrate" (#4).

"Each church gathers regularly to praise and thank God, to remember and make present God's great deeds, to offer common prayer, to realize and celebrate the kingdom of peace and justice. That action of the Christian assembly is liturgy" (#9).

"To speak of environmental and artistic requirements in Catholic worship, we have to begin with ourselves—we who are the Church, the baptized, the initiated. Among the symbols with which liturgy deals, none is more important than this assembly of believers. It is common to use the same name to speak of the building in which those persons worship, but that use is misleading. In the words of ancient Christians, the building used for worship is called *domus ecclesiae*, the house of the Church" (#27, 28).

"The most powerful experience of the sacred is found in the celebration and the persons celebrating, that is, it is found in the action of the assembly: the living words, the living gestures, the living sacrifice, the living meal" (#29).

"In no case, however, should this [consideration of multiple uses of a building] mean a lack of attention to the requirements of the liturgical celebration or a yielding of the primary demands that liturgy must make upon the space: the gathering of the faith community in a participatory and hospitable atmosphere for word and eucharist, for initiation and reconciliation, for prayer and praise and song. Such a space acquires a sacredness from the sacred action of the faith community which uses it. As a place, then, it becomes quite naturally a reference and orientation point for believers. The historical problem of the church as a *place* attaining a dominance over the faith community need not be repeated as long as Christians respect the primacy of the living assembly" (#40, 41).

During these years Hovda was a member of a Catholic community called NOVA, a non-geographical parish in northern Virginia. Here he was able to work with others week by week in putting the principles he wrote about into practice. He frequently presided at the community's Sunday Eucharist.

Two books that Hovda wrote during these years at The Liturgical Conference are significant. The first, *Manual of Celebration*, was both the most practical and the most visionary tool available when the revisions of the eucharistic liturgy were made and a new *Sacramentary* published as the 1970s began. Hovda placed the *Sacramentary*'s texts in one column, then filled the other with his commentary, which was both "how to" and "why." Thousands of priests and liturgy committees used this book step-by-step in preparing themselves and their communities for the revised rites.

Hovda, urged by so many who had experienced both his writing and his presiding at Eucharist, later prepared a book for presiders called *Strong, Loving and Wise*. He wrote about the habits that constitute the art of presiding, the skills the presider needs, the way to think about this work within the Church. A generation later it remains in print.

After leaving The Liturgical Conference, Hovda continued to speak widely. His writing in the final fifteen years of his life took the form of "The Amen Corner" in each issue of *Worship*, the periodical begun by Virgil Michel and published ever since by the Benedictine community of St. John's Abbey. Here he dealt, as he had through the years in *Living Worship*, with a breadth of matters, but ever urging the bond between liturgy and justice, justice both in the Church and in the world. (Many of these essays have been collected by John Baldovin in a volume also called *The Amen Corner*.)

In his last years Hovda would frequently say to friends, especially when encouraged to write more, that he shouldn't be writing or speaking at all because all he did was say the same things over and over, and he just didn't have anything new to say. In a way, he was right. From the Chicago letter to the seminaries requesting admission in 1943, to the North Dakota reflections in the 1950s quoted earlier, and through all the lectures and articles that followed, he grew in eloquence and in breadth as he grew in audience, but the marvelous clarity of his early insights were constant through his life. They needed proclamation as much or more in the thirty years after the Council as those twenty years before.

Any summing up of Robert Hovda's thought would have to do with how he tried to hold together what our institutions keep apart: human freedom and the solidarity of brothers and sisters. We can have one or the other, we are told again and again, not both. Hovda believed that neither freedom nor solidarity had any reality apart from the other, and that Church, precisely church-at-liturgy, was where we are meant to glimpse this, but how hard that is. He believed in the Church, perhaps the way Captain Ahab believed in Moby Dick: forever wed, forever enemies. In a time when it was popular to snicker and walk away from the pathetic institution, Hovda was most articulate in his criticism of the Church and most faithful to it in his life. He didn't leave. He championed the unity of the Church, he sought the dialogue with other faiths, and he did it from the real ground of the Roman Catholic Church. And that Church was, for him, shaped and pounded together, reminded and renewed, in the liturgy that is the deed of the assembled, baptized people.

Three weeks before his death Hovda was preaching this Church that he sought all his life. At a liturgy in Houston he said:

"What is there to rescue us from this idolatry of self and clan? Except worship, except this biblical/liturgical assembly of faith to which we here and now commit our scattered selves again? In our tradition, God trusts us to figure out what all this means, to use our own imaginations to interpret what all this means in our time, our place, our situation. We have no party line—no political, economic, cultural, legal agenda. These things we have to figure out along with everyone else on the planet. What we have in faith and in faith's liturgy is more important: the vision that all politics, economics, culture, and law must be made to serve love and love's reconciling and liberating deeds.

"We are not talking about a reversal of roles, a mere revolution. In this memorial we hear the word together, whether we are rich or poor, female or male, gay or straight, of one color or another, old or young, sick or well, working or jobless, approved or disapproved by our society. All of us whom society tries to keep invisible, for appearance's sake, are made visible here, and not just visible but equal in nobility, honor, calling, love. We wash each other's feet and we share equally a common holy bread and a common holy cup not because we have earned them or are worthy of them, but because of God—blessed by God, whose overwhelming love reduces our silly little human distinctions to trivia, and allows them only because we need each other's gifts and functions to supply a wholeness we can only find together.

"Because we are loved and honored no matter what we have done or have not done, no matter what we have made or not made of ourselves, no matter what our society has done to us in our childhood or of what advantages we have been deprived. We do not have to be ceaselessly examining ourselves or worrying about our past. We have been liberated from the close and stuffy environment of our creation, our world, our culture, into the fresh air of God's reign. From the prisons of my self, my kind, my delusions of superiority, we have been reconciled."

On February 8, 1992, people from every stop Hovda had ever made in his life gathered for liturgy at a church in Brooklyn. Gerard Sloyan told in the homily of a time when Hovda's bishop suggested to him that he should calm down a bit. "You have a messiah complex," the bishop said. Hovda replied: "I thought we were supposed to."

Gabe Huck, writer and lecturer, served on the staff of The Liturgical Conference with Father Hovda. From the late 1970s until July 2001, Gabe directed Liturgy Training Publications in Chicago.

2

The Sacred: Silence and Song

Robert W. Hovda

Catholic common prayer (liturgical celebration, public worship) normally begins with storytelling. As soon as we've assembled, gotten ourselves together as church, as local community of faith, we listen to a proclamation in our midst of the storytellers of the biblical tradition. We name those covenant stories just as we name Jesus: the word of God. The word of God—God's breath, God's will, God's dominion—comes into our community life, freeing us from all the baggage that we ordinarily carry, that we may have been carrying when we entered the ecclesial assembly, freeing us from our ideologies and our statuses: our parties, customs, habits, the structures of our particular status quo, no longer black or white, male or female, straight or gay, capitalist or Marxist, beautiful or plain, handicapped or not. That word comes among us and asserts the priority of the reign of God, the new Jerusalem, what the Scripture calls "eternal life" to which baptism admits us. It provides us with a kind of platform that enables common prayer, whether that prayer is the Great Thanksgiving (the Mass) or the repentance in a celebration of reconciliation or any other rite.

THE MAKINGS OF A STORY

Since we are so accustomed to the priority of storytelling, then, let me begin with a story or, at least, the makings of a story. We could weave the same kind of story, I think, out of almost any period of reform and renewal in the Church or, for that matter, any period in the history of the covenant people, any period when the covenant community was being rejuvenated by the hand of God. Any such period would do, but right now let's weave it out of that unique time when we believe that God's word became visible in our own human flesh, two thousand years ago. Let's go back to Jesus' time for just a minute.

The community of the covenant—the community of the Law and the prophets—had already seen all kinds of ups and downs, stagnations and revivals, punctuating its slow growth and development toward a consciousness of the universality of its mission, a consciousness that the human unity and solidarity found in the one true God is its witness in and service to the world. Even though it was, at that time, oppressed politically, it was still a great institution with a great history. Its synagogue life, its teachers and leaders, its liturgy, what remained of its Temple practices constituted together a mighty fortress against the idolatry of other nations, against all the forces and powers of the world that were, at that time, inimical to faith. Synagogues were probably full, and there were Gentile converts.

This time, when the community's life was so vital, wasn't the time to talk about reform, about a way of life that makes demands beyond those commonly accepted by the faithful. It wasn't the time to talk about changing things, shaking up the covenant community, moving it ahead into the new day that God was revealing. We had a winning organization going, with clear teachings, a neat system, and orderly lines of authority.

Then along comes Jesus. Can't you just hear the leaders of the faith establishment? Even if we didn't have a record of their reaction in the New Testament, you can imagine what it would have been: "This is the time for us to stick together against that common foe, to consolidate, to strengthen the tradition by reaffirming all the customs and the ways that are its glue, to restrain our criticisms, and to form a common front against that Gentile enemy, imperial Rome. It's not the time for asking questions and challenging our ways like that Nazarene is doing." Can't you just hear the faithful: "What is this teacher trying to do? He's taking everything dear and sacred away from us. He's confusing us"—as if confusion were ever the problem. "He's pulling down the traditions and the customs that comfort us, telling us: 'You have made a fine art of setting aside God's commandments in the interests of keeping your tradition.' He is undermining the faith and destroying Judaism." Can't you just hear the theologians: "We have worked hard to make the Torah—the infinite loving kindness of God, the fountain of living water—into a neat, clear, systematized code of rules and regulations, a list of things that people can understand and do. And now this Jesus comes along, exploding our explanations and making questions out of our answers." Can't you just hear the artists, the litterati, perhaps even the musicians: "Is nothing sacred? How can anyone who claims to be from God speak as this Galilean does about the Sabbath and the Temple and our ways of prayer? He is a barbarian who will deprive us of a sense of mystery in worship!"

A SIMPLE MORAL

We could go on with our storytelling, but perhaps that's enough to grasp a simple moral: Don't believe everything you hear, especially don't believe everything you hear from ecclesiastical specialists who are not, first and foremost, believers. It was the ecclesiastical specialists, after all, who were in Jesus' hair from the beginning of his ministry to its end. They couldn't understand the incarnate word any more than they had understood the word of the Law and the prophets, for the word is a profound and interior event, a call from heart to heart. Ecclesiastical specialists, on the other hand, are the machinists of the faith community, whose job is to keep the mechanism functioning, the system going. Unless they are first and foremost believers—a priority that's rarely secure—these ecclesiastical specialists can get so totally engrossed in their system that nothing else matters to them but its smooth operation. Anything that causes a ripple or raises a question or invalidates a custom or appeals to the creative imagination that enables progress, of course, threatens to break down that system and has to be eliminated.

A true believer, one who is first and foremost a believer before he or she is a bishop or theologian or artist or musician, knows what Jesus means when he says: "The Sabbath [or the system] was made for people, not people for the Sabbath [or the system]." A believer knows that the faith community—the Church—is never finalized or finished, never an accomplished fact but always on pilgrimage, seeking, growing, and helping the world grow toward what Scripture calls the reign of God. This faith community comes to realize gradually, with the help of the word of God and the signs of the times, that its ministry in the world is the liberation and unification of the human race, because the God of the Bible is a God who is living, whose creative work is ongoing, and whose call beckons us always to move beyond where we are at any given moment.

Beware, then, the ecclesiastical specialist, whether a pope or a teacher or a musician or a writer, who has a commitment prior to that common commitment of believers. For the ecclesiastical specialist who is not first and foremost a believer, the holy, the sacred, the mystery are identified too easily with a completed system, a finished church, a

17

classic form of art where God is somehow captured and made static, secure as our possession, subject to our control. For such people, the signs of God's great love and saving care—the sacraments—are entities apart from any sordid human grasp, splendid in their isolated and unused perfection.

But, for believers—for the covenant people who are first and foremost believers, that is, all of us no matter our art or craft or trade or specialization or office—the holy, the sacred, the mystery are indissoluble elements of faith and worship: a sense that both causes and proceeds from our common frustration before a radically unknowable God. This is, for believers, the God who is apprehended through the biblical covenants' revelation of divine dominion as something realized progressively through the twin graces of freeing and making one all of the oppressed and diverse peoples of the earth. The holy, the sacred, the mystery are identified by believers with the sole dominion of that God who cannot be captured or possessed, who invites and draws us on a pilgrim struggle and journey that requires us to be dying and rising all the time, to be new persons in Christ Jesus every day. Nourished by our past, certainly, we are called to be focused on today and living now, stripping periodically to the bare essentials of the love of God and of each other, knowing well that what served the covenant community yesterday may not be that which serves its common weal today. In that picture, the signs of God's great love and saving care—the sacraments—are not *things* at all, not static objects but the symbolic actions of our dirty hands, the symbolic deeds of the whole Church that express our faith and make us one in Christ and one with Christ.

We do a profound disservice to the word of God and to ourselves as Church whenever we trivialize that absolutely fundamental awareness and worship of God, whenever we identify the sense of mystery with anything less than the spirit and attitude of a faith community that is supremely conscious of the Holy One. "Hear, O Israel, the LORD is our God, the LORD alone!" Or, in the words of Jesus' tax collector: "God, be merciful to me, a sinner." The status of mystery, of the sacred and the holy that is trivialized by restricted access through an hieratic language or an unintelligible jargon, with the kind of expertise that depends on I.Q. and education, with forms of art perfected in some previous age or culture, with any (however subtle) effort to escape from *hoi polloi*—that sense of mystery is, from a believer's point of view, ersatz, phony, and ultimately self-defeating.

One of the great European Catholic intellectuals of the early twentieth century, Friedrich von Hügel, said something about this in the florid style of his time, in a letter to a niece. His niece had written to him about her disappointment with church services; about her attraction to what she called "the best"; about her opinion (which, I am sure, I share and most of us do) that most churches, now as then, were middling, dull, and repulsive in their public worship. Von Hügel answered his niece, who was named Gwen, without defending the churches she described. He carried no brief for the second-rate or for carelessness (nor should we). Instead, he responded with these lines:

"The touching, entrancing beauty of Christianity, my niece, depends upon a subtle something which all of your fastidiousness ignores. Its greatness, its special genius, consists, as much as in anything else, in that it is without this fastidiousness. A soul that is, I do not say tempted, but dominated by such fastidiousness, is as yet hovering around the precincts of Christianity. It has not entered its sanctuary, where heroism is always homely, where the best always acts as a stimulus toward helping, toward being, in a true sense, but one of the semi-articulate, bovine, childish, repulsively second-, third-, fourth-rate crowd. So it was with Jesus himself; so it was with Francis the *Poverello*; so it is with every soul that has fully realized the genius of the Christian paradox. When I told you of my choking emotion in reading in St. John's Gospel that scene of Jesus, the Light of the World, as the menial servant at the feet of those foolish little fishermen and tax gatherers, what do you think moved me but just that huge life- and love-bringing paradox, here in its fullest activity. The heathen philosophies, one and all, failed to get beyond your fastidiousness. Only Christianity got beyond it, only Christianity. But I mean a deeply, costingly realized Christianity got beyond it. Gwen will some day get beyond it. It's really a very hideous thing: the full, truly free beauty of Christ alone completely liberates us from this miserable bondage."

A CHANGE OF POSTURE

Together for common prayer with the Bible and the cross, to face the Holy One with that kind of intentionality, is to create a scene that enables a change of posture for those involved. This is the point of the holy, the sacred, the sense of mystery: a change of posture, a change from being the one in control, the one in charge, to being the worshiper; a change from being the user and exploiter to being the reverencer and lover; a change from being the one who has to have all the answers to being the one who is comfortable with mystery and questions; a change from being the master to being the seeker. That's where holiness is experienced—there, at that deep level—and I think only there.

This is not all that I want to say on this topic, far from it. But this is prior and basic to everything else. Unless we recognize that the experience of the sacred and the holy and mystery begins at this deep level of faith, of God-awareness, then we doom all of our efforts. What von Hügel called "fastidiousness" and what many contemporary Americans call "good taste" is a particular cultural value that has absolutely no significance at the universal human and spiritual level to which we must descend when we are talking about the holy.

Only after we face that basic truth can we talk about other things—and we must talk about other things, for humans are always people with particular cultures and with a great variety of gifts and talents and sexes and colors and classes and educations and lifestyles. It's in our particular context, with all of this great variety, that we have to try to serve the deep and fundamental change of human posture that I've described here.

A FEW PRACTICAL CONSEQUENCES

What can we do, in our respective contexts, to encourage, enable, and nourish that experience of the holy? Most readers of this essay find themselves involved regularly in practical problems of liturgical planning and celebrating in their own communities. If what I have said so far is as fundamental to the experience under discussion as I think it is, then it should have clear relevance to our work in planning and celebrating. I'm not a musician, but I have devoted most of my adult life to just these questions, so let me draw out just a few of the practical consequences of these convictions.

First, such a conviction about the holy means trying to understand the depth of the reform which was made the business of the whole Church by the Second Vatican Council and never, never, never allowing ourselves to be so myopic and so hypocritical that we apologize for the greatest event-gift God has given us in medieval or modern times. Whatever backward or forward fads and fancies come over us and our sisters and brothers; whatever backward or forward popes and bishops and pastors and other leaders we elect, ordain, or receive; whatever backward or forward pressures we get from elitists who are understandably attached to this or that archaic form, our beginnings of reform—though they are still just beginning—are certainly on the path of the best-equipped renewal in the history of the biblical covenant. (It is the best-equipped in terms both of the Church's liturgical, scriptural, patristic studies and of the world's scientific and technological advances.) We are just beginning, as a consequence of this reform, to realize again what church life always is supposed to be: a quest and not a hanging-on for dear life. So we cannot be surprised at the cries of pain: Attachments, like all idolatries, are familiar problems for believers. To be faithful to the covenant, it seems to me, is simply to have no doubt about where our responsibility lies, and that is in pushing the reform ahead with everything we are and have.

Now to three practical aspects of the nascent reform that are particularly relevant and challenging for pastoral musicians and others involved in serving the Church's liturgical life: its rediscovery of conversion, initiation, and baptism as the constitution of the Church and the foundation of specialized ministries like ours in the Church; its rediscovery of the symbolic, artistic, body-language nature of liturgical celebration; and its rejection forever of the kind of petrified book-liturgy which governed Catholic worship from Trent until Vatican II.

The rediscovery of initiation as the root of all ministry tells us, as musicians and other ministers involved in the service of the churches, that we are finally beginning a very slow process of outgrowing that unspoken but implicit division of the Church into a gnostic elite of leaders with God-connections that are inaccessible to most and the majority of the faithful, who must experience the holy secondhand. That division was a temporary reversion, a bit of atavism in our history, but it lasted for a long time. The great identification with Jesus Christ and with the priesthood of Jesus Christ is again, now, baptism and not holy orders. So the entire assembly is the primary minister in liturgy, and the variety of specialized ministries, which we are in the process of rediscovering again in our life as Church, are all in the service of the assembly, dependent in many ways on that assembly. Sacraments are no longer things that the priest brings to the rest of us but rather symbolic actions that we all do together. We need offices of ministry for the doing of them, to be sure, but they are our common actions, with the different roles that a liturgical assembly requires.

Therefore, we ask questions that we didn't think of asking when the church building was regarded as a service station for individual Christians rather than as the gathering place of the faith community. The multiplication of Masses on Sunday is a beautiful example of how necessity is the mother of corruption. Somewhere along the line, in our history, we had to ask for a second Sunday eucharistic celebration to accommodate our growing numbers, because you couldn't just go and start a new parish every time you burst the seams of the room you were in. This reluctant concession to necessity, once established, became the norm, and now we think there's something wrong if we don't offer a separate Eucharist for every different time schedule, for every available clergy person (as if the Mass were for the priest and not the priest for the Mass), for every different private need. Now, we know again that the gathering of the sisters and brothers *together* is a primary sign in the Sunday assembly, a primary part of the symbol.

That awareness means both shaking up and simplifying our Sunday schedules and reexamining the spiritual and economic practice of daily Mass. It also means that if our ministers are no longer gnostics and gurus, then their specialized service to us, both in liturgy and in the rest of our community life, has to be based on talent and training and the call of the community. We might think, what a novel idea, but that's the way God calls. Archbishop Weakland of Milwaukee says that when a person asks him how to become a church musician, he answers: "First, become a musician." The Church simply has to begin to take talent and training seriously again as qualifications for any specialized ministry. We know how much we owe to people who volunteered when no one else was around or stood up to offer their services, but we have relied for far too long on volunteers, goodwill, private feelings of call, and rites of public commissioning or ordination to supply what only talent and training and time can supply. This means radical changes in recruitment, training, lifestyle, as well as qualifications not just for musicians but for all of our specialized ministries, including bishops and priests.

Most of all, perhaps, this vision of the holy means an economic reorganization of church life, the like of which we have never seen before. To demand talent and training and sufficient time for functioning—for doing the job—we have to begin paying ministers realistically, and we have never had to do that in our lives or in the whole of church history (though there may be some hidden period in which we did this that I am unaware of). That's why, no matter how much talent and training anyone has, one would have to be independently wealthy to be able to *volunteer* as much time as the ministries require.

It's a gigantic project, so we may have to begin in small ways, by tending to particularly critical ministries, like that of music, first. Like all other liturgical ministries, the ministry of music requires a lot of time for preparation, for practice—more time, in fact, than most of the other ministries in the Church, with the possible exception of the presider's ministry. Further, all such preparation and practice—by the musician as by all the other ministers—has to be done *before* the rite, so that from beginning to end of the celebration the minister is one with the rest of the assembly in attending to every moment of the action. It's terribly destructive of common prayer when the music director or one of the vocal or instrumental musicians—or any other minister, including the clergy—does not participate by attending to the proclamation of a reading or a vocal prayer or whatever ritual action is occupying the assembly at the moment but seems simply to be preparing for the next piece of music or the next action in which that person has a role in leadership. All ministers of liturgy have to be, first of all, participating members of the assembly: That's crucial.

When we look at the second of the rediscoveries or aspects of the current reform, the rediscovery of ritual's native language, we come up against a double cultural problem. We are heirs of a European church culture that has vastly overemphasized the intellectual, the rational, and tragically diminished our sense of the importance of body, imagination, fantasy, senses, memory, feelings—the non-verbal and non-cerebral levels of human communication. We are diminished in precisely the areas that liturgy needs most. The diminishment that factor represents is compounded by the fact that we are also heirs of a capitalist, technological, pragmatic, also narrowly intellectual and production-oriented culture of the West in general. Anything, therefore, that does not seem to contribute either to our knowledge or to our productivity is suspect. No wonder we've been so embarrassed for centuries by the generous proportions of the liturgy's traditional symbol- and body-language, so embarrassed by it that we've allowed it to shrivel up to almost nothing, to be desiccated by the dry winds of rationalism and verbalism.

Now the reform asks us—pleads with us—to open up the symbols of our tradition so that music, furniture, vessels, environment, gesture, movement, posture, vesture—all these materials and elements—come into their full communicative power, so that they do not have to be rationally or verbally explained but can communicate with all the power that is in them when they are set free. We need to have all the sense experience we can have of everything associated with the breaking of the bread and the pouring of the cups, with the sharing of Holy

Communion through eating and drinking in procession, with getting the sisters and brothers together for a really *festive* Sunday celebration, a special occasion: the acting out of the reign of God in contrast to all of the oppressive and divisive factors of our daily life, dominated as it is by our military, political, and economic institutions. Let us spend our time and our money and our energy in doing everything we can in a human way and with the human arts for that gathering, that celebration of the new Jerusalem where everyone is sprinkled, everyone is blessed with incense, everyone is kissed, everyone is honored—that celebration which helps us feel so good about ourselves and our world, so important, so dignified, so precious, so loved, so free because it lifts our hearts with its transcendence-bearing-beauty to love the God who makes us free and one. Our limits and our sins impose so much ugliness on our world; public worship has to try to reveal its beauty in every way it can.

Music in liturgy, in this context, is therefore not an adjunct or ornament, any more than any of the other human arts brought into our ritual play as a mere adjunct. Music is a way in which we pray. Nature and God's human gifts conspire in music to praise the holy. Music is itself prayer; whether it has a text or not, whether there any lyrics or not, music is prayer. Trivial music, therefore, or sentimental and self-serving texts insult a people who are in quest of the holy, who are trying to leave behind their roles of self-sufficiency, self-centeredness, and control to assume the posture of a worshiper, a reacher for that which is beyond our grasp, beyond the stars, a seeker for the meaning that is the foundation of all created things. No human art or power is adequate to this reaching, so nothing will do but our very best efforts and talents, given our own cultural context. We have to win back to the service of the faith community all those artists whom we have alienated for generations. No art form is sacred in itself, but all are sacred. All are inadequate and limited, as we are, but we and they are nonetheless claimed by Christ.

Think about the challenge to music and the other arts that liturgy affords, if we understand it in this way. Think about how the arts can develop and blossom and grow beyond our dreams in such an environment of searching and reaching.

Alexander Schmemann, the Orthodox theologian, suggests that one of our problems is that our rationalist and a-liturgical tendencies in this culture have made the world grace-proof by dividing reality up and then opposing the parts: natural vs. supernatural, sacred vs. profane. He illustrates this by talking about the simple act of blessing water. That act, he says, may have two totally different meanings. The first is that the act of blessing water may be considered the transformation of something "profane," and thus religiously void or neutral, into something "sacred," in which case, the main religious meaning of "holy water" is that it is no longer mere water and is, in fact, opposed to it. In this view, the sacred posits the profane as religiously meaningless. Or the act of blessing water may be considered, as it is deeply in our tradition, as a revelation of the true nature of water and, thus, of the world: an epiphany and fulfillment of nature's sacramentality. In this view, the blessing restores and reorients water by putting it consciously in the context of prayer, in the context of God's dominion, of God's reign, as part of the priestly act of a priestly people. The blessing asserts the relation of water to God: "Holy" water is revealed as true, full, adequate *water*, and matter, once again, becomes a means of communion with God. Reform is moving us from the first view to the second, but very, very slowly (almost imperceptibly).

The arts have no safe and secure forms that were made eternally valid at some imaginary super-sacred moment in our past. The arts have to stretch to serve a living Church that is, once again, on pilgrimage and on the move, just as we all have to stretch to be part of such a Church. We can use the great creations and compositions of the past when they are appropriate to a living and developing public worship, but never to retreat, only to inspire the march.

It is as creation itself and for its sake that the assembly of the converted and baptized gather in their symbolic acts of faith before the one, true God, to become the locus of the holy, the sacred, the mystery. What the faith community does is what makes the building or the environment sacred in a special way. That's what makes any art it uses sacred in a special way. That's what makes for an epiphany of the natural as sacred, just as we become ourselves most fully and holy in worship. "To God what is God's": That is the whole of us. So all else in nature experiences the same blessing and orientation. Only in blessing God are we blessed.

Finally, the last aspect of reform that I mentioned is the rejection of book-liturgy. Those who are old enough may remember the days when the only thing you needed to be a leader in public worship was to have the book in hand. Everything was there, down to the last detail. Now the liturgical books are totally different—not as different as they will be, but totally different from previous volumes, nonetheless.

They offer us the rich structures and the skeletal outlines of a long tradition that is still being made, with options aplenty, with pastoral adaptation a requirement awaiting our flesh and blood, our arts and letters, all the talents and imagination we can summon, all the experience of the mission in which the baptized (presumably) have been engaged. Those liturgical structures are right; they have clear patterns from gathering, through building up, to climax, to dismissal in some relatively standard forms.

Those are the things musicians have to work with now. There are no more neat little patterns to follow, no more *Kyrie, Gloria, Credo, Sanctus, Agnus Dei.* Now we have a summons to creative gifts and talents in the service of a living worship that needs acclamatory responses for eucharistic prayers (maybe more of them than we have so far); that needs meditative or acclamatory responses for the readings; that needs processional songs for entrance and communion; that needs inspiring music for moments when the rest of the assembly listens, as at the sprinkling or at the preparation of the altar and gifts or at other times; litanies for petitions at the breaking and the pouring; and so on. The whole scene is new and to be explored. That is not a reason for complaint; it should be a cause of joy for artists. Indeed, it is such for artists but not for copyists.

And we need silences. Perhaps musicians and clergy need to remember this especially. We need lots of silence; we are in desperate need of silence. I do not mean intervals or intermissions or pauses to catch one's breath or find one's place. I mean extended periods of silence, period, which, in this context, is silent prayer. The various rites indicate a number of appropriate places for silence. The point of the Mass at which I have found extended silence to be most rewarding and most easy to accomplish communally is after the sharing of Holy Communion and before the prayer after communion, When everything stops, and all are seated, and voices are stilled, and songs are stilled, and instruments are stilled, and movement and gesture are stilled, there is no prayer more eloquent than silence. Like music, silence is itself prayer. It takes time and repetition to get into a practice like that, but it's worth the embarrassment of first efforts. Persistence pays with the possibility of an experience of the holy that is free of the limitations of our culturally conditioned art forms.

Finally, I really believe that in almost everything, especially in liturgy and our experience of the holy and our cultivation of a sense of mystery, less is more: less quantity, more quality; less frequency, more significance; less ordinariness, more impact; less busyness, more purpose. As the Gospel song says, "Keep a-inchin' along, Jesus'll come by and by."

Rev. Robert W. Hovda, a presbyter of the Diocese of Fargo, died in the night of February 4–5, 1992. This article is based on an address that Father Hovda delivered during the 1982 NPM Regional Convention in Providence, Rhode Island.

3

Liturgical Prayer: Twenty-Five Years of Change

Virgil C. Funk

Change is universal and constant—it happens to everything and to everyone. The dramatic changes in the Catholic Church since the Second Vatican Council have saturated every form of Catholic life. Here, I examine three areas—our parish assemblies, our songs, and, especially, the pastoral musicians. On the occasion of the 25th anniversary of the National Association of Pastoral Musicians and my retirement as President, these three areas provide a clue to the vision and challenges that lie ahead of us.

ASSEMBLY

A wide range of writing on parish assemblies exists—from a theological view, from pastoral practice, and from a sociological view of community. My approach draws on these perspectives, but I invite you to reflect with me specifically on how singing and our songs have transformed our communities. What follows are seven observations about song's influence on assemblies in the past thirty-five years:

1. When we invited the assembly to go from silence to song, we invited them to exchange their role as observers of the rite for that of shared ministers in the rite.

2. When we invited the assembly to sing specific ritual songs, the assembly moved from participant in shared ministry to primary worshiper. As soon as an assembly reflects on the truth that it is the Church, the Body of Christ, that worships the Father, everything begins to change. And music participation, in the minds of the council fathers, was one of the primary ways in which change was to be effected. In our times, the continuing democratic revolutions begun in our own nation in 1776 and in France in 1789 have clashed with the remnants of European hierarchical thinking. That clash is how the Vatican Council

was interpreted in the U.S.; nowhere is it more visible than in the quest for "full, conscious and active participation" . . . through song.

3. When we go from Gregorian chant to multilingual celebrations, we are moving from the basic ritual monastic model of St. John's, Collegeville, Minnesota, to the pluralistic model of Sunday Mass in the Archdiocese of Los Angeles. Think of the change from a presumed homogeneity of Dubuque, Iowa, in 1960 to the celebrated multicultural Los Angeles of 2001. We are and always have been a Church of many cultures and tongues. In 1960 some of us celebrated in ethnic parishes: Polish, German, Irish, and the rest. Today, however, when multilingual repertoire is sung in almost every parish, we are transforming through music the parish's understanding or image of itself. (The effect of these ritual transformations are explored in this volume in the articles by Jan Michael Joncas and Nathan Mitchell.)

4. Architecture shapes our identity. When we went from Gothic churches with pews stretched down elongated naves to churches in which everyone gathers around the altar (*"circumstantes"*), facing one another in some form of confrontational seating, not only did the new shape of our buildings affect the acoustic of the singing but, more importantly, it affected the "direction" of our text. The text of worship has developed a tendency to move from an almost exclusive singing directed to the transcendent (to the "other"—whether that is God the Father, the Virgin, or the saints) to singing to the Christ incarnate in the body assembled. This singing in turn has reinforced or transformed our principal understanding of worship's direction. And the theologian of this change is most often the musician who has control over the variable texts in the liturgy: the so-called "soft spots."

5. From 1965 to 1975 pastoral ministry was centered on implementing changes that were new to pastor, musician, assembly, even bishop. In 2001 we are dealing with maintaining models of participation during leadership transfers and transformation; we are also dealing with overcoming bad musical experiences stemming from poor implementation. Poor repertoire or, more often, good repertoire performed poorly turned certain parishioners either to permanent silence or to open resistance against any further effort at assembly song. Some young people are naively longing for an imaginary ideal time before the reform experienced by their parents. This transformation has moved from singing that is fresh and new, to singing that is political, to singing that is downright offensive.

6. We have gone from a common, shared experience of musical liturgy in the 1940s to a wide diversity of musical experiences that vary from parish to parish, diocese to diocese. The *Liber Usualis*, in use from 1907 to 1965, shaped a common experience of what *liturgical* music was, but, more important, what *liturgy* was. The *Liber* contained the basic celebrative model and created a common experience. My experience tells me that the Southwest is different from the South, which is different from the Midwest, which is very different from the East Coast. And the repertoire that is used, as well as the way it is performed, differs significantly from region to region. Without a basic celebrative model and a common experience, we learn by doing. *Lex orandi statuat legem credendi*: How we pray shapes what we believe. By our diverse singing, we believe in diversity of belief.

7. We are in the process of transformation. I have written extensively about this elsewhere; to summarize: What we have done in moving from "singing anything" to singing Protestant hymnody, both adopted and adapted, to singing new compositions by the St. Louis Jesuits, the St. Thomas More Group from England, the Taizé community in France, has influenced everyone's understanding of pastoral music's power to transform. We learn by doing; if you live outside the U.S. Catholic pastoral experience, however—either because your worship community is isolated from the mainstream or you live in Rome or another place outside our country—you fail to understand fully the transformative power of music as it is experienced in everyday pastoral practice in the parish.

SONG

Not only has the assembly been transformed by the singing, but the song itself has been transformative. A number of people have done a musical analysis of this transformation, especially Elaine Rendler and Fred Moleck. My own contribution is not in the area of musicology or musical theory but theology, and my focus is on how our theological understanding of music has changed and how our pastoral practices have changed our theological understanding of music.

What follows is an abbreviated presentation of an article I wrote that appeared in the *New Catholic Encyclopedia* (2001) under the heading, "Liturgical Music, Theology and Practice." This article examines nine documents in the context of an unfolding pastoral implementation of the liturgical reform: the *Constitution on the Sacred Liturgy, Musican sacram* (1967), The *General Instruction of the Roman Missal*

(1974; rev. 1982), *Music in Catholic Worship* (1972), the *Universa Laus Document* (1980), *Liturgical Music Today* (1982), *Plenty Good Room* (1990), the *Milwaukee Statement* and the *Snowbird Statement*.[1] No doubt you recognize the different types of documents:

- from the council: the *Constitution*;
- from the *Consilium* (the ad hoc committee responsible for implementing the decrees of the council concerning liturgy under the aegis of the Congregation of Rites, later the Sacred Congregation for Divine Worship): the statement *Musicam sacram* and the first edition of the *General Instruction*;
- from the Catholic bishops in the United States, either as a body or through their committees: *Music in Catholic Worship, Liturgical Music Today*, and *Plenty Good Room*;
- and from groups of musicians: *Universa Laus*, the *Milwaukee Statement*, and the *Snowbird Statement*.

Each set of documents has significantly different authority, but all have influenced in some degree our understanding of ritual music. Examining what these documents have to say about the theology of music and, to some extent, their impact on pastoral practice provides us a perspective on the thinking since 1965 and contextualize our present legislation.

A. Ultimate and Proximate Ends

The Constitution *Sacrosanctum Concilium* clearly established music's purpose or "ultimate end"; that is, it identified music's place within the general purpose of all liturgical action, which is to associate the church with Christ in the "great work wherein God is perfectly glorified and the recipients made holy" (CSL #7). The end of liturgical music, therefore, is "the glorification of God and the sanctification of

---

[1] These source documents may be found in English translation in the following publications. The *Constitution on the Sacred Liturgy, Musican sacram* (1967), The *General Instruction of the Roman Missal* (1974; rev. 1982), *Music in Catholic Worship* (1972), and *Liturgical Music Today* (1982) are available together in *The Liturgy Documents: A Parish Resource, Volume One*, third edition ed. Elizabeth Hoffman (Chicago: Liturgy Training Publications, 1991). The *Universa Laus Document* (1980) appears in Claude Duchesneau and Michel Veuthey, *Music and Liturgy: The Universa Laus Document and Commentary*, trans. Paul Inwood (Washington, D.C. [Portland, Oreg.]: The Pastoral Press, 1992). *Plenty Good Room* (1990) may be found in *The Liturgy Documents: A Parish Resource, vol. Two*, ed. David A. Lysik (Chicago: Liturgy Training Publications, 1999). The Milwaukee Statement and the Snowbird Statement have both been published in *Pastoral Music*: 17:1 (October–November 1992) and 20:3 (February–March 1996), respectively.

the faithful" (CSL #112; see *Musicam sacram* [MS] #4). Diverse interpretations of how music is to accomplish this end have developed in the Catholic Church during the whole twentieth century, before and after the Second Vatican Council. One approach, for example, focuses on an incarnational ecclesiology: By becoming fully human, one achieves the completion of humanity's goal and reaches, through divine grace, participation in the divinity of God. Another holds that by transcending normal experience through participating, for example, in an aesthetic experience, one is lifted toward union with the divine.

The *function* of liturgical music—how it moves toward achievement of its ultimate end—has also been debated in the context of these approaches. In the official documents, the function (*munus ministeriale*) has been stated in various and diverse terms, reflecting the differing approaches to the theology of liturgical music that influenced those people developing a particular document. One such approach would maintain that the elements of holiness, beauty, and universality are key elements of any art used in the liturgy to achieve the transcendent goal of the act, so they are also required of the musical art form used in liturgical worship. Another would maintain that "sacred music will be more holy the more closely it is joined to the liturgical rite" (CSL #112). In short, there are disagreements even in the official documents regarding liturgical music's function or "proximate end."

The council's liturgical document had the development of full, conscious, and active participation of the whole assembly as "the aim to be considered before all else" (#14). Because of existing documents and practices in 1963, however, encouragement of new compositions (#121) in accord with the above goal took second place to promotion of music from a treasury containing products of ages that, compared with the theology of liturgy articulated in the *Constitution on the Sacred Liturgy*, do not represent an ideal in theological-liturgical thinking. That tension between the liturgical theology articulated at the council and the recommended musical practices to express that theology did not take long to reveal itself.

B. Tensions

The tension between the council's theology and its recommended practice, in fact, surfaced quickly in 1966 at two meetings of liturgical musicians in the United States. The Fifth International Congress on Sacred Music of the Consociatio Internationalis Musicae Sacrae (Milwaukee and Chicago, August 21–28) brought musicians from other nations into contact with U.S. liturgists and musicians for the first time since the council. Later that year, a joint meeting of the Liturgical Conference and The Church Music Association of the United States (November 29–December 1, Kansas City, Mo.) brought together North American liturgists and musicians representing two approaches to liturgical music. Both meetings were marked by heated exchanges.

Abbot (later, Archbishop) Rembert Weakland, O.S.B., who chaired the U.S. Bishops' Advisory Board on Music and who was present at both meetings, challenged the participants by saying, "We cannot preserve the treasures of the past without coming to terms with the false liturgical orientations that give birth to this music, nor can we preserve them according to the false aesthetic judgments of the last century." American musicians took up the challenge, whether they were classically trained composers such as C. Alexander Peloquin and Richard Proulx, ethnically based musicians such as Rev. Clarence Joseph Rivers, or popularly oriented writers such as Joe Wise and Carey Landry.

C. Clarification

The growing struggle over correct application of the council's principles did not go unnoticed by the Vatican. On March 5, 1967, the Sacred Congregation of Rites issued *Musicam sacram*, the only postconciliar document specifically on music to be issued for the universal Church. Its purpose was to provide clarification regarding "some problems about music and its ministerial function" (*munus minsteriale*, #2). *Musicam sacram* first reiterated the transcendent and imminent purpose of music, "for the glory of God and the sanctification of the faithful" (#4); then it expanded the definition of "sacred music" by including both Gregorian chant and sacred polyphony as well as the "sacred, i.e., liturgical or religious, music of the people" under one heading (#4). Such music is used, the document said:

- to provide a more graceful expression to prayer;
- to bring out more distinctly the liturgy's hierarchic character and the specific make-up of the community;
- to achieve a closer union of hearts through the union of voices;
- to raise minds more readily to heavenly realities through the splendor of the rites;
- to make the whole celebration a more striking symbol of the celebration to come in the heavenly Jerusalem.

Previously, in *Tra le sollecitudini* (1903), Pope Pius X had described the functions of sacred music as holiness, beauty, and universality, which produce an art form. In *Mediator Dei* (1947), Pius XII stated a more emotional and eschatological function:

"A congregation that is devoutly present at the sacrifice, in which our Savior together with His children redeemed with His sacred blood sings the Nuptial Hymn of His immense love, cannot keep silent, for 'song befits the lover,' and, as the ancient saying has it, 'he who sings well prays twice.' Thus the Church militant, faithful as well as clergy, joins the Hymns of the Church triumphant and with the choirs of angels, and all together, sing a wondrous and eternal Hymn of praise to the most Holy Trinity" (#192).

A close reading of the functions named in *Musicam sacram*, in comparison with these earlier statements, especially Pope Pius XII's evocation of the divine nuptial song and the heavenly liturgy, shows how the list of functions reflects an understanding of music that has shifted from Pius X's extraliturgical measure of liturgical music as an art form to the more intraliturgical understanding of music as "the more holy the more closely it is joined to the liturgical rite" (CSL, #112). In addition, *Musicam sacram* added a third element to the discussion, clearly influenced by pastoral practice: "The choice of the style of music for a choir or congregation should be guided by the abilities of those who must do the singing"(#9).

D. General Instruction of the Roman Missal (1975 edition)

The revised *Ordo Missae* of Pope Paul VI and the accompanying *General Instruction of the Roman Missal* (GIRM) were first published in 1969, with a revised edition appearing in 1975. Unhesitatingly, the GIRM affirmed that "great importance should be attached to the use of singing at Mass" (#19). The instruction describes the function or purpose of each section of the liturgy, following it with a set of practical instructions on how that function is to be expressed. By establishing a ritual function followed by the celebrative model, the instruction provides not only specific directives about what should be done but establishes the criteria by which the ritual act may be judged to be accomplished or not. Each element of the liturgy is similarly described in the instruction. Slowly and deliberately, these principles guided the creative development of the rite, freeing it from a false rubrical rigidity.

E. Pastoral Practice

From the mid-1960s pastoral practice was seeking ways to implement the flood of directives and texts. Publishers were developing repertoire, experimentation took place everywhere, marked by little or no guidance. Those who had been informed of good pastoral practice through participation in the Liturgical Weeks sponsored by The Liturgical Conference numbered fewer than five hundred leaders and fewer than fifty thousand one-time attendees. One cannot underestimate the size of the task faced by the churches after the council or the minimal number of persons prepared to take on the task of implementing the council reforms in the North American Church.

F. The Influence of Music in Catholic Worship

In 1972, the U.S. Bishops' Committee on the Liturgy issued the statement *Music in Catholic Worship*, confirmed by the full conference of bishops (the National Conference of Catholic Bishops, now the U.S. Conference of Catholic Bishops) and revised in 1983. This document established a theology of music based on a theology of celebration:

"We are Christians because through the Christian community we have met Jesus Christ, heard his word in invitation, and responded to him in faith. We gather at Mass that we may hear and express our faith again in this assembly and, by expressing it, renew and deepen it (#1).

"Interior and exterior participation are understood as aspects of one act: 'We are celebrating when we involve ourselves meaningfully in the thoughts, words, songs, and gestures of the worshipping community—when everything we do is wholehearted and authentic for us—when we mean the words and want to do what is done' (#2).

"And boldly, echoing Pope Pius XII and subsequent documents: 'People in love make signs of love, not only to express their love but also to deepen it. Love . . . must be expressed in the signs and symbols of celebration or [it] will die' (#4).

"Perhaps the most challenging statement for practicing musicians and for other liturgical ministers appeared in #6: 'Good celebrations foster and nourish faith. Poor celebrations may weaken or destroy it.'"

Of all the documents addressing music in the decades immediately after the council, *Music in Catholic Worship* had the most significant influence on the North American theology of music and its practice because it was profound and practical, and it engaged the American religious imagination. It also offered a threefold practical judgment as a way to "determine the value of a given musical element in a liturgical celebration" (#25). Three aspects characterized the judgment: musical, liturgical, and pastoral. Is it good music? Does it relate to the liturgical function? Does my community sing it? For the Catholic

Church in the United States, in fact, this was the first document to deal with inculturation.

As a result of the widespread influence of *Music in Catholic Worship*, pastoral practice began to shift. Whereas some communities had been invited to sing *anything* at the key processional moments of entrance, preparation, and communion (plus a closing song), now music was more often chosen in accord with the threefold judgment and an initial understanding of its ritual function. Additional attention was being paid to music with texts rooted in the Bible, especially to new responsorial psalm settings. In many parishes, communities began to sing the *texts* of the liturgy—especially the psalm and Gospel acclamation and the eucharistic prayer acclamations—"singing the liturgy" as compared to the practice in many places that could be described as singing "at the liturgy."

G. Modified Pastoral Practice

During this time—in the mid-1970s—the influence of pastoral practitioners on the development of our understanding of sacred music cannot be underestimated. In these years, people began to use the Scripture-based and more musically sophisticated works of such composers as the St. Louis Jesuits, and the National Association of Pastoral Musicians began to gather and provide a voice for practitioners charged with leading sung worship in parishes Sunday after Sunday.

The churches in this postconciliar period faced several practical tasks: (1) to develop a repertoire in the vernaculars used in the nation; (2) to teach the whole assembly—the congregation as well as its ministers—to participate; and (3) to participate in the revision of the average parishioners' notion of God, the Church, sacraments, and their own baptism. These tasks made use of and reshaped the theology of liturgical music.

Combining theory with practical experience, these leaders of musical liturgy began to use *Music in Catholic Worship's* musical-liturgical-pastoral judgment as a guideline for each parish community. Internationally, though this guideline was not expressed by other hierarchies as it had been by the U.S. bishops, this threefold judgment in effect became the standard by which development of liturgical music was measured, though its application was influenced in various nations by tendencies in the national culture. So, for example, the German Catholic community, with its history of great composers, from Bach through Beethoven and into the modern era, and its familiarity with great musical literature, instinctively approached the task of congregational singing through the use of quality music organically related to its tradition as uppermost in its musical consciousness. The French, on the other hand, with a strong background in contemporary scriptural and liturgical scholarship, enthusiastically took on the task of relating the music to the liturgy and began to emphasize music's ritual function, for which new compositions were required. The Americans, characteristically, took a pragmatic approach, asking: Does the assembly sing it? These different approaches reflect an emphasis on one or another aspect of the threefold judgment as well as an understanding of music for the liturgy as "sacred," "liturgical," or "pastoral."

H. An International Attempt at a Theology of Liturgical Music

In 1980, Universa Laus, an international group for the study of singing and instrumental music in the liturgy, published a report of its work since its formal organization in 1966. This *Universa Laus Document* provides a wealth of information regarding the developing theology of Christian ritual music in the twenty-five years after Vatican II. The overall theological premise of Universa Laus regarding ritual music is stated in the following terms:

Christian worship consists of:
a. the proclamation of salvation in Jesus Christ;
b. the response by the assembly of believers; and
c. the making real, by action, of the Covenant between God and humankind.

Music is integrated into these different components of worship:
a. to support and reinforce the proclamation of the Gospel in all its forms;
b. to give fuller expression to professing one's faith, to prayer (intercession), and to the giving of thanks; and
c. to enhance the sacramental rite in its dual aspect of action and word (*UL*, "Points of Reference" 1.2).[2]

I. Liturgical Music Today

The statement *Liturgical Music Today (LMT)*, published by the U.S. Bishops' Committee on the Liturgy in 1982, was an attempt to articulate principles governing the function of music in the liturgy and the function and form of various musical elements (# 6-11). In fact, *Liturgi-*

[2] Duchesneau and Veuthey, *Music and Liturgy*, 15.

cal Music Today provided practical directives for new situations that had arisen since the publication of *Music in Catholic Worship*.

LMT proposed a new understanding of the traditional repertoire and its use. Rather than commending it as high art and therefore as the most appropriate music for Roman Rite liturgy, *LMT* placed this repertoire in the context of historic faith and worship: "Singing and playing the music of the past is a way for Catholics to stay in touch with and preserve their rich heritage. A place can be found for this music, a place which does not conflict with the assembly's role and the other demands of the rite" (#52). A blend of music from the past and new music composed for congregational participation was proposed as both a pastoral ideal and a practical application of liturgical music's function (*munus ministeriale*).

On the matter of music ministry, *LMT* began with a theological statement that would have been highly controverted just twenty years before: "The entire worshiping assembly exercises a ministry of music" (#63). The document then turned its attention to pastoral practice by addressing the musicians in terms of a theology of their ministry:

"Some members of the community, however, are recognized for the special gifts they exhibit in leading the musical praise and thanksgiving of Christian assemblies. These are the pastoral musicians, whose ministry is especially cherished by the Church.

"What motivates the pastoral musician? Why does he or she give so much time and effort to the service of the Church at prayer? The only answer can be that the church musician is first a disciple and then a minister. The musician belongs first of all to the assembly; he or she is a worshiper above all. Like any member of the assembly, the pastoral musician needs to be a believer, needs to experience conversion, needs to hear the Gospel and so proclaim the praise of God. Thus, the pastoral musician is not merely an employee or volunteer. He or she is a minister, someone who shares faith, serves the community, and expresses the love of God and neighbor through music" (#63–64).

J. Broader Influences

In these years pastoral practice in the United States was influenced by more sophisticated composition and by a wide range of styles in musical repertoire. The British St. Thomas More Group, with Christopher Walker and Paul Inwood, brought to the U.S. a new level of craft in popular pastoral music. Together with U.S. composers J. Michael Joncas, Marty Haugen, and David Haas, they introduced into the liturgy music techniques from secular culture, especially from Broadway-style musical forms. More classical forms were also being reshaped based on a renewed liturgical theology and pastoral practice. These included attempts at a new style of chant for use with English texts. Richard Proulx's *Community Mass* and Marty Haugen's *Mass of Creation* began to create an "American standard" for common eucharistic acclamations. A wide range of styles, setting the texts of responsorial psalms, was being published, though most compositions followed the pattern of providing an antiphon for the congregation with verses for the cantor or choir. In these years, as well, despite the wealth of new materials, liturgical music practice was beginning to stabilize in many parishes.

K. American Attempts at a Theology of Liturgical Music (1990 to 2001)

Though *Music in Catholic Worship* (1972) may be considered the first document to address liturgical inculturation for the Catholic Church in the United States, the first document to address the multicultural challenge to worship in U.S. Catholicism appeared in 1990. *Plenty Good Room: The Spirit and Truth of African American Catholic Worship* (*PGR*, August 28, 1990), produced by the Black Catholic Secretariat of the United States Conference of Catholic Bishops, contained reflections on music in the Black church. It notes especially that people of African-American heritage "do not sing only to make music" (#3).

Like most of the American Catholic documents, *PGR* affirms liturgy's symbolic nature: "First, one cannot arbitrarily make symbols—they are not merely things. They become symbolic because of their resonating with the members of a given historical, cultural, ethnic, and racial community. They can assume levels of meaning that make sense of birth, life and death—by means of tradition, community and grace" (#5). *PGR* applies the following symbolic understanding to liturgical music:

"A person may be particularly moved by the singing of a certain hymn . . . Were they asked, 'what do these symbols mean?' they respond, 'I don't know. I didn't even know they were symbols.' This would not imply that they have not experienced meaning in their symbolic activity. They have, for symbols are truly multi-dimensional phenomena" (#9).

In other words, the measure of successful repertoire is not whether a particular piece is a "hit" but whether it succeeds in the order of religious symbolism.

The function (*munus ministeriale*) of African-American sacred song, as Sr. Thea Bowman noted, is holistic, participatory, real, spirit-filled, and life giving. She describes those characteristics this way:

- Holistic: challenging the full engagement of mind, imagination, memory, feeling, emotion, voice and body;
- Participatory: inviting the worshiping community to join in contemplation, in celebration, and in prayer;
- Real: celebrating the immediate concrete reality of the worshiping community—grief or separation, struggle or oppression, determination or joy—[and] bringing that reality to prayer within the community of believers;
- Spirit-filled: energetic, engrossing, intense;
- Life giving: refreshing, encouraging, consoling invigorating, sustaining.[3]

L. The Milwaukee Document

A group of composers, liturgists and theologians met for ten years in Milwaukee (1982–1992) at the suggestion of Sr. Theophane Hytrek, S.S.S.F., and under the sponsorship of Archbishop Rembert Weakland, O.S.B. On July 9, 1992, they issued *The Milwaukee Symposia for Church Composers: A Ten-Year Report (MS)*. This document brought to the attention of musicians in the United States the elements connected with Christian ritual music and contained in the Universa Laus document. It also sought to describe a theology of ritual music, since it affirmed that "a theology of Christian ritual music is necessary." While such a theology "may be implicit in some of the official documents," *MS* stated, "there has been little explicit attempt in these documents to fashion such a theology" (#10). According to the statement, the basic elements from which to construct such a theology include:

- Music as sound, the raw material of music, reveals God in a non-localized, symbolic way (#13).
- Music is rhythmic and, therefore, time-bound; it "underscore[s] the temporality of human existence into which God has intervened" (#14). In this temporal aspect, music becomes one with the very nature of the liturgy.

[3] Sr. Thea Bowman, "The Gift of African American Sacred Song," in the preface to *Lead Me, Guide Me: The African American Catholic Hymnal* (Chicago: GIA Publications, 1987) [v].

- Music heightens words. Because word reveals God in the liturgy, music has a heightened role in the liturgy (#15).
- Music uniquely unites "the singer with the song, the singer with those who listen, [and] singers with each other." It is therefore a sacramental symbol of the mystical body at prayer: "The song of the assembly is an event of the presence of Christ" (#16).

M. The Snowbird Statement

The American dialogue on the purpose and function of music in the liturgy continued with the publication, on November 1, 1995, of a statement by a small group of liturgists and musicians meeting in Utah. Titled *The Snowbird Statement,* this document entered into dialogue with the *Milwaukee Symposia* report and current pastoral practice. *Snowbird* affirmed the category of ritual music as an appropriate way to describe music in the liturgy, but it warned against reducing that category to a kind of practical functionalism.

Many of the points made in *Snowbird* are based on the premise that there is a Catholic liturgical "ethos":

"Still we believe that a Catholic ethos is discernible, for instance, in music that elaborates the sacramental mysteries in a manner attentive to the public, cosmic and transcendent character of religion, rather than in styles of music that are overly personalized, introverted or privatized."[4]

Those who seek a concrete example of the tension that still exists in the legislation, in various statements about the liturgy's music, and in pastoral practice and in the Church today, need only reflect on how the Eucharist is celebrated on any Sunday in neighboring parishes in any diocese and, sometimes, in liturgical celebrations within the same parish. Various "schools" are represented, few liturgies embrace any one approach exclusively or in totally consistent ways; therefore, everyone who participates will probably experience some "disconnect." There is, in fact, no master model of liturgy that is applied consistently in pastoral situations in the United States.

In summary, both in theory and in practice, judgments about liturgical music have gone from evaluations of reperotire judged on artistic merit and, in an external way, to judgments about music that serves as a means for expressing ritual function and, in some people's minds, as

[4] "The Snowbird Statement on Catholic Liturgical Music," *Pastoral Music* 20:3 (February–March 1996) 15.

an act of revelation of God, the Almighty. We have moved, in other words, from judgments and choices external to liturgy to those based within the liturgy itself, in both its functional aspects and its ultimate purpose.

THE TRANSFORMATION OF THE PASTORAL MUSICIAN

After examining the transformation that has occurred in the assembly and its music, I turn to the transformation that has taken place in the pastoral musician. It is my fundamental belief that good musicians make good music, though the musician's role in liturgy has always been underestimated, overlooked, or presumed.

But you know about the transformation of the pastoral musician because you know about the transformation that has taken place in your heart. You know about your conversion to faith, your struggle with musical competency. You know about your sense of vocation informing everything you do, including your music making. You know about your call from God and how it has transformed you. At the core of the National Association of Pastoral Musicians is that call to transformation.

You also know about the external transformation of our image: from organist for the weekday *Requiem*, invisible to the parish from a perch in the choir loft and underpaid, to the director of music ministries or, more often, the musician-liturgist: the one responsible for liturgical prayer in the life of the community in collaborative ministry with all other ministers, including the bishop. Or is that second part of the vision yet to be realized? I would contend that we are actually part way there, so we are moving from the invisible organist to the more visible musician-liturgist.

Just as we have moved from "sing anything" to "ritual music which functions to fulfill the celebrative model of the rite," so too, we have moved from "anyone can make music" to the reality that liturgy requires us to become certified, competent musicians. We know that excellence in all areas—liturgical, musical, and pastoral—is essential to our ministry because good signs enrich faith and bad signs can destroy faith. The transformation of the pastoral musician is written on every page of *Pastoral Music,* on every gathering of the Association, and in the hearts of every true pastoral minister.

A Summary of Three Transformations

We now have a grasp of the essential elements of the current picture: The major sections are covered in broad strokes by the image of the assembly which has been transformed from passive spectator to participating minister, to principal worshiper—a process in which the experience of music has assisted.

In the middle ground of this painting, we see that our music has gone through a transformation of understanding: from a romantic aesthetic describing music's artistic transcendence to a functional aesthetic that describes its ritual role as revelatory of the presence of God and the preparation for the coming of the reign of God.

In the foreground we find ourselves: pastoral musicians who have progressed from organists playing the weekday *Requiem* and accompanying evening novenas, to directors of music ministries responsible for liturgical, musical, and pastoral judgments that affect the faith life of the assembly and therefore of the Church. (Of course, we know that these positions are reversed in liturgy: the musician is in the background and the whole assembly is in the foreground.)

THE VISION AND THE FUTURE

A. A Vision Described in Themes

A quick review of our national conventions' themes provides a view of the transformation of our vision over the past twenty-five years.

- Our first convention heralded the conviction that *Musical Liturgy Is Normative*; that is, it is normal that the rite be sung. We also affirmed that musical *Prayer* is a combination of *Performance and Participation*. If there is too much or too little of either, the prayer collapses; it turns into entertainment, self-serving sing-a-long, liturgical opera or, even worse, an ill-performed amateur hour.
- Musical liturgy is a unique art form, different from fine art or folk art, and existing as a musical form before both opera and radio music existed. *Claim Your Art!* Don't imitate any of the other musical art forms that exist, because none of them is identical to what you do.
- Our art form *Remembers into the Future*—we use music in the present to remember specific events of revelation in the past in order to prepare us for the eschaton and Christ's coming. There are three revelations in our music: past, future, and present.
- Music makers are blessed with a gift of music, the first sign of the vocation, the call from God. But music makers are called to serve in the parish in which they find themselves, perhaps with inadequate instruments or imperfect acoustics or even less than perfect co-ministers. (At least we always have a perfect community, ready to join the musician in sung prayer.) *Blessed Are the Music Makers!*

44

- Our vision includes all believers. Quoting the prayer in the *Didache*, we affirm: *"As Grain Once Scattered* on the hillside is made into one bread, so too from all lands your church will be gathered." Music unites; in the past thirty years, the emergence of a common Christian repertoire has taken place—often at our direction. The efforts at ecumenical music-making must continue to grow parish by parish, event by event.
- Our vision is about hope. Just as important as the gift of hope, however, is another gift that music provides: an ability to cope—with sorrow, grieving, loss, failure, separation. *How Can We Keep from Singing,* even when we feel loss, whether it be the personal loss of a friend or the loss of the vision of renewal. We are the champions of hope for others and for ourselves. We sing in the face of adversity. "Even at the grave," the Eastern Churches remind us, "we sing *Alleluia.*"
- Central to our vision is the need to *Sing a New Church* into being through a new ecclesiology of participation, a new theology of God incarnate, a new understanding of ministry. Some question whether this vision is new or simply the addition of new verses to an old song. "You don't put old wine into new wineskins," our Scriptures tell us. Jesus did envision change. As the prophet says, God is doing a "new thing; now it springs forth, do you not perceive it?" (Isa 43:19).
- Our vision is about liturgical time: the celebration of the Church's feasts and seasons. Our melodies, along with our liturgical texts, speak of *The Rhythm of the Church Year,* a reality central to our work.
- Our vision is about justice—we sing about the *God of Justice Who Knows No Favorites* (Sir 35:12, NAB). Because ours is an incarnate faith, we also hope for justice in the larger world, in our work, and in our lives. We are committed to world peace and justice—and to justice for our ministry.

As we review these themes of our gatherings—liturgy, prayer, artistic excellence, remembrance and preparation, ourselves as music makers, ecumenism, hopefulness, ecclesiology, the Church year—we sense our movement toward transformation, remembering that it is God's power, not our own, that we invoke to transform us and our world.

B. The Future—the Documents

Our history as an association shows we have stayed with the vision for the past twenty-five years. But what can we say about our immediate future and our long-term future?

Remarkably, for the first time since the years immediately after the Second Vatican Council, there are five official liturgical documents in process at this time. They include a new edition of *The General Instruction of the Roman Missal (IGMR 2000)* and the Latin text of a new missal, which has been promised for a year and was still, in 2001, expected, plus the revised American appendix to the *General Instruction*. There are also two new statements by the U.S. bishops: *Built of Living Stones*, on the relationship among liturgy, art, and environment, and *This Holy and Living Sacrifice*, guidelines regarding Communion. The most recent of these documents is the *Fifth Instruction on the Implementation of the Constitution on the Sacred Liturgy of the Second Vatican Council*—on the use of vernacular languages in the publication of the books of the Roman liturgy, issued by the Vatican's Congregation of Divine Worship.

While none of these documents is entirely new, they do contain new materials that set the agenda for our future. A key issue for musicians centers on the recommendation in the *Fifth Instruction* that a new translation of Sacred Scripture be developed with an emphasis on the original texts but with a significant role assigned to the Latin *Nova Vulgata* translation as normative in cases of debate.[5] This translation, if completed, will probably have a bearing on the texts used in our music that are drawn directly from the Scriptures—the responsorial psalm, for example.

Further, IGMR 2000 and the *Fifth Instruction* place significant importance on creating a translation of the other liturgical texts that accurately reflects the Latin of the Roman Missal, with special emphasis on the texts of the entrance, presentation, and communion song (see IGMR 2000, #392; *Fifth Instruction*, #60–61). At the present time, the American Appendix to the current *General Instruction* provides for wide latitude in usage for these processional chants, as long as the ritual function of the rite is preserved. In speaking with the leadership working to provide a sense of direction in the area of music in light of these documents, I hear a desire to maintain an effective balance between drawing our musical texts used in the liturgy closer to the Latin liturgy and an awareness that our congregations are singing much

---

[5] See the Congregation for Divine Worship and the Discipline of the Sacraments, *Fifth Instruction for the Right Implementation of the Constitution on the Sacred Liturgy of the Second Vatican Council* (Sacrosanctum Concilium, art. 36): *On the Use of the Vernacular Languages in the Publication of the Books of the Roman Liturgy (Liturgiam authenticam)*, March 28, 2001, nos. 34–38. See also IGMR 2000, no. 391.

more than is contained in those official texts. In other words, so far as processional music in the United States is concerned, the toothpaste is already out of the tube.

In addition to the challenges and opportunities provided by the new documents, here are a few more challenges that I see before us as pastoral ministers.

We are challenged to recognize that "freedom" in North American culture has led to great gains, especially in the area of inculturation. At the same time, freedom has pulled us farther from the Latin sources and has reinforced among American Catholics a sense of individualism—and, from the point of view of the larger world—of arrogant superiority among Americans generally. We are eight percent of the world population, yet we consume forty percent of the world's resources; we also resist being curbed by the world's will on such matters. Those of us with worship responsibilities, then, will be challenged to maintain a liturgical experience for the assembly that is counter-cultural and faithful to the Gospel message.

We are challenged in the manner of Cyril and Methodius, who brought the Byzantine liturgy to the Slavic world through a process of translation and inculturation, to maintain essential ties to the root liturgy and at the same time develop a relevant liturgy for the community.

We are challenged to teach our musician members to play our repertoire well, accurately, and beautifully. We are a long way from developing in every parish the musical skills necessary for the minimal celebration of the Missal of Paul VI.

We are challenged to continue the education of our clergy members in the best liturgical practice, based on sound teaching and valid experience. We are challenged to name and support our best parish experiences and foster their expansion.

We are challenged to work with parishes who have had poor experiences of music, to heal the wounds and to step back and listen to what is being said by the disillusioned. We need to learn to maintain a relationship with those people with whom we disagree. We need also to find constructive ways to maintain liturgical awareness in communities that experience leadership transition, whether that be maintenance or the transition center on the parish pastor or, to some extent, on the music minister.

We are challenged to find ways for everyone in music ministry to obtain support and encouragement in the their ministry, without reinforcing inadequacies. While I do not think we need "professionals" in every parish, we surely do need competencies in every parish.

We are challenged by the fact that the U.S. liturgical movement of the 1940s through the 1960s has landed on our doorstep. In North American churches, pastoral musicians are the instruments through whom liturgical implementation is taking place. Our challenge will be to maintain our commitment to the ideals of the Second Vatican Council, tempered by the experience of Sunday parish celebrations. We know the song "Sons of God" is inappropriate *now*, yet many in the 1960s sang it with enthusiasm. What songs are we singing enthusiastically today that will be critiqued, in turn, by our deeper understanding of liturgy and music?

We are challenged to maintain our roots in the biblical renewal. Central to my own understanding of the liturgy was my training in Sacred Scripture. The primary sources of revelation are the Scriptures and the liturgy. We will be challenged to expand our awareness of the Scriptures, of their meaning and interpretation based on modern techniques and the tradition of the Church.

A Profound Influence

The theology of church music and its practice have profoundly influenced the period immediately following Vatican II. More Christian believers have participated in the practice of church music in these years, as ministers and as members of the singing assembly, than in almost any other era of church life. A perfect solution to the task of linking the treasury of sacred music to the requirement for assembly music has not been found, but many are aware that such an organic link is beginning to develop. An agreed-on theology of ritual music does not exist, but efforts have been made to begin the process of developing such a theology. A new repertoire for assembly participation, while not complete, is well on its way. Pastoral practice is by no means stable, yet considerable effort has been made toward a workable model. The Church is currently being served by a large core of competent musicians, skilled at the craft of assembly song. The theology of liturgical music and the pastoral practice associated with it will continue to develop as we strive to make music for the glory of God and the sanctification of the faithful.

Rev. Virgil C. Funk, a presbyter of the Diocese of Richmond, is the founder and president-emeritus of the National Association of Pastoral Musicians.

4

Ritual Transformations:
Principles, Patterns, and Peoples

J. Michael Joncas

In this article I look at how the changed religious rituals of Roman
Rite Catholics have transformed Catholics over the past twenty-five
years, especially from the perspective of the rituals' nonverbal communication: their subtexts or paratexts. First I'll suggest five principles
arising from the study of religious ritual. Then I'll explore in-depth
with you three changed patterns of ritual behavior in our Roman Rite
Eucharist, contrasting how we celebrated them according to the
Missale Romanum 1570 right up until 1962 and how we've been celebrating them according to the *Missale Romanum* 1970 for the past thirty
years or so. Finally, I'll suggest some transformations in attitude and
devotion probably in dialogue with the changes in the ritual that participants have gone through.

FIVE PRINCIPLES ABOUT CHANGE IN RELIGIOUS RITUALS

1. Complex religious ritual systems develop by adopting, adapting
or rejecting elements of other religious systems.

While researching the worship patterns of ancient Jews, Greeks, and
Romans as the presumed matrix from which primitive Christian worship arose, I discovered that what we perceive as Christian creativity
in worship actually consists in adopting, adapting, or rejecting those
other religious traditions. An easy example of adoption appears in the
Christian custom of praying with hands upraised: what we call the
orans position. This posture is frankly simply stolen by the primitive
Christian community from Jewish prayer. Statutory Jewish prayer
called for a standing position: At prayer you were ʿ*Amidah,* the just
ones who stood upright on the good earth on your two feet. You didn't
crawl on your belly in the dust like the condemned snake; you stood
upright when you prayed. And you lifted your hands in *yadah,* in testimony, before God. So much was this position ingrained in Jewish

prayer that the *berakoth,* recited three times a day by pious Jews, normally called *Shemoneh ʿesre* or Eighteen Benedictions are popularly referred to as the *ʿAmidah,* the standing prayer. With such background, we begin to see how important the posture is.

Now, in contrast to adoption, adaptation can be well illustrated by the Roman Rite custom of carrying lit candles and incense before the Gospel Book. In Roman imperial secular custom, those of senatorial rank had the right to be preceded through the streets of Rome with slaves carrying torches and incense. Given the non-sanitary and odoriferous character of Roman alleys, even today, it would, of course, make sense to have light to see where one placed one's feet and sweet scents to mask the smell of animal excrement and human refuse. So these were originally practical necessities—they weren't marks of rank. But over time they became marks of social status: Only certain people were permitted to walk behind what might otherwise be of practical use to all citizens: Only senators and those of higher rank could be preceded by slaves with the lights and the incense.

What did Christians do with this practice? Not only did the Christians adopt the practice, substituting acolytes for slaves and bishops for senators, but they also adapted it for their public worship. As an inanimate object the Gospel Book does not need to be protected from stinky sewage as it is carried in solemn procession through a basilica—the basilica also being an example of Roman civic architecture adopted and adapted by Christians. But since the Evangelary was perceived as being a special mode of Christ's presence, the honors given to senator and bishop were lavished on the book.

Rejection of cultural patterns can be seen in the Christian development of Advent. Where pagan Roman culture celebrated a Saturnalia festival of gastronomic excess and sexual fun, Christians fasted and worshipped. As the Roman pagans performed their excessive ritual behavior in contrast to the waning of the sun, Christians were called to fast: Rather than the gastronomic excess of the *ululatio,* they would embrace a gastronomic minimum and celebrate the feast of the Unconquered Son.

So, to summarize this first principle: Complex religious ritual systems develop by adopting, adapting or rejecting elements of other religious systems. We should not be surprised, therefore, that Christian worship has adopted, adapted and rejected elements of ancient Jewish, Greek, and Roman worship. What may really come as a surprise, however, is the fact that presently the Roman Rite continues to interchange with all sorts of cultures throughout the world, adopting, adapting, and rejecting certain elements of contemporary culture.

2. Complex religious ritual systems carry meanings that may enshrine, modify, or subvert meanings enunciated in the texts.

There's a catch phrase in counseling psychology: What you are doing speaks so loudly that I can't hear what you're saying. I distinctly remember while in college a rather surreal moment in a philosophy class where our professor, dedicated to showing us the faulty reasoning in Marxist dialectic materialism, grew red in the face with the veins popping out in his neck, as he pounded on the desk, shouting: "And under no circumstances must a philosopher become passionately involved in his argument, lest he lose his objectivity!" What he was doing, of course, spoke so loudly that the text he was trying to communicate just disappeared. Now, in my middle age, I really look forward to being behind cars with a bumper sticker that says, "Question authority," so I, safely behind the wheel of my car, can mutter: "Yeah, who are *you* to tell me?" How easy it is for language to turn on itself; how easily context transforms text.

These considerations lead to this illustration of my second principle: the gesture in our present practice of receiving Holy Communion in the Roman Rite. The minister of Communion extends the consecrated host or broken consecrated bread toward the recipient and declares, "The body of Christ." I suspect if we were to poll most recipients and ask, "What does this mean?" they would say, in these or other words: "The gesture enshrines a declarative understanding of the text: This is the body of Christ." This interpretation of the gesture and its statement is so widespread that, at least in the United States, a fair number of eucharistic ministers have taken it on themselves to add those words to the text: "Oh, Heather, this is the body of Christ." (Of course I'm going to bracket here the discussion of this metaphoric interchange, since the one thing that should be obvious to both the minister and the recipient is that the consecrated host is *not* the body of Christ in exactly the same way as blood, bones, and organs were the body of the historical Jesus.) There is a wisdom, however, in the ritual's refusal to make this text a declarative statement, because then the gesture may modify the *denotation* carried by the text with rich, symbolic *connotation*. The "body" announced by the text may have as its first referent the consecrated host, but it also carries the connotations of the minister's providing and the recipient's receiving, the common eating and drinking, the processional activity of those coming to and moving away from common eating and drinking: All of these are the body of Christ. These connotations depend on how the minister and recipient make eye contact, what tone of voice the minister uses, how the recipient articulates "Amen," and whether or not the host is placed in the hand or on the tongue.

Subversion of meaning occurs, for example, when a minister of Communion recites the text not before but while placing the consecrated element on someone's tongue or in the hand. It narrows the connotations. When a minister distributes consecrated hosts in a rushed or hurried manner—like distributing cards, when a recipient snatches rather than receives the host, or when the recipient simply neglects to respond "Amen," thus refusing the ritual engagement: (saying, by such behavior, "I'm here for Communion, I'm not here to talk to you"), do such actions or inactions then shatter the experience of Communion?

As a consequence of this principle, I would judge that the communicative potential of religious ritual works best when the context for proclaimed texts is congruent with the denotative and connotative meanings borne by the texts and, conversely, the communicative potential of religious rituals breaks down when the context subverts the meanings borne by ritual texts. This principle may be footnoted for pastoral musicians with this observation: Applying this principle means that you can't have a one-size-fits-all music program for all the liturgies on a given weekend. At five o'clock on Saturday afternoon, you can't ask the congregation to rise to its feet and sing: "Holy, holy, holy, Lord God almighty, early in the morning our song will rise to thee." If you do that at five o'clock on a Saturday afternoon, the clear context says: "Actually, God, we aren't doing that now; that song is going to rise to you tomorrow morning." Context, in other words, can subvert text, even when the text is sung.

Margaret Mary Kelleher has done liturgical studies a great service by distinguishing among official, public, and private meanings attached to religious ritual.[1] As I understand her, she would say this: First, official meanings are those enshrined in formal documents and magisterial pronouncements; they attempt to provide a universal rationale for the maintenance and continuation of a ritual. Second, public meanings are those explicitly expressed or implicitly assumed by the ones actually participating in the ritual. They're not enshrined in

[1] Margaret Mary Kelleher, "Liturgical Theology: A Task and a Method," *Worship* 62 (1998) 2–25; see also Margaret Mary Kelleher, "Hermeneutics in the Study of Liturgical Performance," *Worship* 67 (1993) 292–318.

books; they're enshrined in people's activity. These meanings are held in common by the celebrating group and justify their participation in the ritual. Third, private meanings are those idiosyncratically associated with the ritual by a participant. Although they might derive from the official or public meanings, they may also supplement or block such meanings. Kelleher's distinctions among these official, public, and private meanings lead to our third principle.

3. Complex religious ritual systems bear official, public, and private meanings that may cohere, inform, or contradict each other.

To illustrate this, I would like to consider a wedding procession in a Roman Rite marriage celebration of two Catholic Christians. The official meaning of the wedding procession is articulated in the *Ordo Celebrandi Matrimonium:* Let those representing the Church, namely, the officiating minister and assistants, meet those covenanting marriage, namely, the bride and groom, the witnesses, the parents, and, while the entrance song is sung, let them together move to the place where the biblical texts will be proclaimed and preached.[2] That's the official description. In fact, the ritual book offers two different formats for this act of entrance—one in which the couple is met and welcomed at the door by the officiant and assisting ministers, who then conduct them with their witnesses and parents to the ambo area, and a second ritual format in which the couple, accompanied by their witnesses and parents, go to the ambo area, where they are met by the official ministers who are already present.[3]

What I want you to observe is that nowhere in the official ritual format does the pattern most familiar to United States Catholics ever appear, namely, the officiant with assisting ministers going into the sanctuary; the male attendant escorting a paired female attendant in procession as the best man, and groom appear at the side of the sanctuary while the maid or matron of honor, walking alone, and the bride, escorted by her father (or another male relative), walk down the center aisle to meet up with the male comrades with whom they will be paired.

What is the public meaning of this common pattern, which ignores the required order of the official ritual? It can be traced back to matrimonial customs in antiquity: The bride, as chattel property, is being

---

[2] See the *Rite of Marriage* (1969) nos. 19–20, or the *Ordo Celebrandi Matrimonium* (1991) nos. 45–46.

[3] See the 1969 Rite, loc. cit., or the 1991 *Ordo*, nos. 48–50.

transferred from the control of the first male responsible for her, namely, her father, to the control of the second male who will be responsible for her, her groom. But when I have asked brides who choose to begin their weddings with this gesture whether they are aware of this rather demeaning public message, in which they are identified as chattel property to be passed from one male to another, they answer: "No, what this does is gives me a chance to have a special moment with my Dad."

Here we have an official, a public, and a private meaning all converging. What do we as pastoral musicians do? Do we say, just for starters, that "Here Comes the Bride" is not the most appropriate music to accompany this entrance procession, nor is Mendelssohn or Pachelbel? The official text says that the entire assembly is singing songs at this beginning of the covenant of marriage; current U.S. practice generally suggests that the assembly watch what is, to all intents and purposes, a small parade rather than an entrance procession as we would understand that a Mass—a parade that is to be watched and, therefore, accompanied by instrumental music, since the congregation can't watch the action and look at a hymnal at the same time.

As a consequence of this principle, I would hold that the communicative potential of religious ritual is fostered when public meanings derive from or at least don't contradict the official meanings. In the example I have just considered, if a distinctive, official meaning in Christian matrimony is the radical equality of the spouses, then a public ritual that suggests that one of the spouses is the possession of the other spouse is going to be problematic. I would also hold that the communicative potential of religious ritual is fostered when private meanings derive from or at least don't contradict the official and public meanings. Here, one might suggest that both sets of parents accompany their children, thus communicating the radical equality of the spouses, the marital witness provided by both sets of parents, and an opportunity for intimate contact between the persons being married and their parents. Put it another way: If the bride takes flowers to the Virgin, the groom had better take lilies to St. Joseph.

So, conversely, the communicative potential of religious ritual declines when official, public, and private meanings are in conflict or opposed.

4. Human ritual activity activates different portions of our neural network. Therefore, human ritual activity is irreplaceably bodily.

Earlier studies of ritual behavior evidence anthropocentric and logocentric biases. Much scholarly ink has been spilled trying to distinguish human ritual from repetitive animal behavior as well as trying to distinguish human ritual behavior from other forms of human behavior. In fact, ritualizing seems to be an activity that humans share with animals, especially primates.

Many studies also approach ritual as a particular way of encoding thought—some viewing it as infantile or neurotic behavior that was going to be outgrown by enlightened rationality. That was the approach taken by Freud: The kind of neurotic activity exhibited by someone washing their hands over and over and over again is just like going to Mass every Sunday—they're both infantile and they're both meant to be outgrown.

Others see ritual as primitive attempts to manipulate the environment—a futile exercise that should be replaced by the more effective application of scientific technology. What we do now, for example, is understand the meteorological conditions and send up planes to seed the clouds to cause rain rather than, as a group of Native Americans might, dance in thanksgiving and jubilation because it rained, and then flip the causal relationship: Let's dance in order to make it rain. Those following this approach would say that ritual is just bad technology, a technology that you dispose of once you understand how the world really works.

Still other observers study ritual as a system of nonverbal illustrations of what could be communicated much more precisely in verbiage. In fact, as Catherine Bell has taught us, theories of ritual frankly seem to mirror the assumptions about ritual made by the investigators much more than the rituals they're studying![4]

Nathan Mitchell has consistently called our attention to the biological roots of human ritual behavior. In an article in *Worship* he suggests that we have three brains: a reptilian brain responsible for keeping our hearts beating, our lungs breathing, and our temperature tolerable; a mammalian brain, also known as the limbic system, responsible for our pre-rational, emotional response to stimuli; and a neocortical brain responsible for abstract reasoning.[5] Each has a role to play in human ritual behavior. The reptilian brain guarantees that no matter how carried away we are by the "Hallelujah Chorus," we're still going to have blood flowing through our veins and oxygenated blood from our lungs' activity; our intestines are going to be keeping up their peristaltic

[4] Catherine Bell, *Ritual Theory, Ritual Practice* (New York: Oxford, 1992).

[5] Nathan D. Mitchell, "The Amen Corner: Ritual as *Ars Amatoria*," *Worship* 75 (2002) 250–259.

motion even if we're in the midst of musical rapture. In contrast, the mammalian brain is especially involved in the artistic and emotional dimensions of our ritual, triggering activist responses to stimuli and prolonging moods prior to and sometimes in opposition to our rational thought. As an example, think of those parishioners for whom the simple sight of a thurible—even if it doesn't carry any charcoal or the charcoal isn't lit, and there's no incense burning in it—will trigger a mammalian brain response of coughing.

Finally, our neocortical brain empowers our ability to synthesize sensate data into coherent structures to employ imagination and memory and fantasy, to judge the correctness of our interpretations of reality, even to think about our thinking and evaluate our evaluating. In a word, our neocortical brain engenders what we identify as the meaning or the theme of our ritualized behavior. Think about the favorite pastime of liturgists and musicians: sharing stories of your five worst liturgical experiences, complete with an annotated bibliography of why the experiences were so terrible. (I sometimes image music ministers lighting up cigarettes moments after every liturgy concludes, sighing, and saying: "It was a pretty good Eucharist for me. How was it for you?")

Mitchell's investigation reminds us that the attempt to understand religious ritual in terms of meanings or themes is to remain quite literally on the surface of the experience. Neocortical ruminations on ritual behavior are necessary and helpful, but they do not unlock the mysterious power of the ritual. The mammalian brain is hardwired or imprinted to respond with deeply ingrained feelings and moods to sensory stimuli.

A friend of mine, who is a priest chaplain in San Diego with the military, had a recurrent pattern of dreaming at one point in his life that he identified as his "God dream." In the dream he was conscious of being surrounded by white—not a blinding whiteness but a featureless expanse stretching off as far as he could see. He knew himself to be alone with this whiteness, but he did not feel frightened so much as puzzled. As he continued in the dream to look over this amorphous, featureless whiteness, he began to have a primal connection with a speaking voice addressing him. He couldn't make out the meaning—he couldn't hear any words—but he was aware that the voice was addressing him. Larry associated this dream with his understanding of God: God is a transcendent, featureless power completely surrounding and sustaining him, a power that addresses him in mystery.

Thinking that he might be developing into a mystic, Larry shared this recurrent dream with his spiritual director, and she—trained in both psychology and spiritual direction—told him to ask his parents if he'd ever had the croup as an infant. And if so, what treatment his parents had used. His mother told Larry that he had had a rather severe case of the croup during the first year of his life and that she had followed the pediatrician's instructions to put a humidifier at the foot of his crib and cover the crib completely with a white sheet to concentrate the effects of the medicated air. Now the doctor had told the mother that Larry might feel scared and abandoned by such a treatment, so in order to reassure him, she was supposed to sing or talk to him from the other side of the blanket while this treatment went on.

I tell this story not so much to disclose the true meaning of Larry's infant memories but to illustrate how pre-rational attitudes and moods can be stored in the mammalian brain. A secular reductionist might conclude that all religious discourse can ultimately be traced back to such primal memories, that humans are simply haunted by infantile experiences, and, once you understand them, you have to reject religious faith—it's just hoohah. Interestingly, though, even after Larry made the connection between this early experience of being treated for the croup and his so-called "God dream," the rational insight—the neocortical stuff—did not cause the dreams to stop, nor did Larry abandon contemplative prayer practices. A person of faith, you see, counters a secular reductionist by saying it is God who employs our neural hardwiring to encounter us. Recall the Thomistic principle: Whatever is received is received according to the mode of the recipient, not according to the mode of the giver.

This leads me back to my fourth principle: Human ritual activity activates different portions of the neural net and is irreplaceably bodily. There is a world of difference between notional apprehension that one is a forgiven sinner and the experience of forgiveness expressed and encountered in two contrasting patterns of ritual in the sacrament of reconciliation. In the Roman Rite pattern, especially in its older form, a penitent enters a darkened room, lists his or her sins in number and kind, and hears through a translucent screen a male voice declaring that you are absolved. That's a very different ritual experience from that provided in the Byzantine Rite, in which a penitent stands side by side with the confessor, both facing an icon of the merciful Christ, with the confessor putting his hands on the penitent's shoulder and wrapping the penitent with his priestly cloak, bringing the penitent under the mercy of the Church. Then, in this ritual, the priest asks the penitent before Christ, "Have you done this?" "Have you done this?" "Have you done this?"—to which the penitent replies yes or no. Then comes the conclusion: "Well, now, as both of us stand before the merciful Christ, I declare to you with complete conviction and authority, in the name of the Church, 'He never stopped loving you, no matter what you did.'" Do you hear how different the rituals are in articulating the same neocortical insight that we are forgiven sinners?

There are forms of prayer that attempt to transcend our bodily condition, but Christian liturgy is not one of them. As a consequence, there is no such thing as a virtual liturgy, however much our friends at EWTN or in cyberspace chat rooms might want to claim otherwise. Liturgy happens when bodies meet each other in space, not when you take pictures of other people doing things in space.

5. Finally, while religious authorities can prescribe official ritual patterns and provide official rationales for them, they cannot control the public and private meanings inhering in the enacted rites.

Ritual activity is not so much brainwashing as a performative zone of contestation. The easiest example I can think of to illustrate is the development of new community postures and gestures during the recitation or singing of the Lord's Prayer in Roman Rite Eucharist. Although this pattern appears in no official liturgy books, many American congregations, over the past twenty-five years, have spontaneously begun to move out from their pews as the priest addresses them with the ritual invitation to pray, join their hands while the text is recited, remain standing with their hands joined while the priest prays the embolism prayer, and then lift hands for the doxology before they let go of each other's hands and return to their places for the rest of the Communion rite.

There are many intriguing things about this. First, there is no official sanction for it, but there's nothing in the rite forbidding it. It is neither *contra legem*—against the law, nor *pro lege*—done according to the law; it's simply *praeter legem*—outside or apart from the law. Christian communities have come up with something new.

Second, the pattern seems to have originated in small-group Masses celebrated by particular groups like charismatics or base communities or other self-selecting communities and then imported into parish Masses. The surprising part of this development, of course, is how little resistance there's been to it in the larger communities or at official levels.

Third, the change in posture from simply holding hands to lifting them marks a clear distinction between the first three sections of the text—the invitation, the Lord's Prayer, and the embolism—and its final section, the text of the doxology. But notice that there's no attempt at a gestural choreography illustrating the movement of thought enunciated by that entire text.

Fourth, the joining of hands highlights the communal, verbal performance of the prayer. Such gesturing would have been inconceivable forty years ago. Some of us are too young to know this, but some of us can still remember that, when we used the former form of the Mass, the priest prayed the Lord's Prayer, and the only text the community had was the very last phrase—*"sed libera nos a malo."* There was no doxology at all. *Sed libera nos a malo:* The only part of the prayer that we had, if we understood the Latin text, was a petition—"Deliver us from evil." You can understand the different between joining in that text and ritual act of community praying the entire text and then gesturing it doxologically.

Fifth, the subtext of this gesture emphasizes the unity of the assembly and the praise of the God who unifies them. That's certainly one of the thematics elements of the Communion rite, but it underplays other thematics, such as the eschatological waiting for God's reign or mutual forgiveness of sins: those elements aren't being gestured. Prayer for protection—another theme—is not being gestured. Finally, when liturgical scholars have suggested that this hand-holding-and-lifting gesture be replaced, that the entire congregation would more suitably stand in *orans* position, since that of course is our ancient Jewish heritage—in effect mirroring the priestly gesture—this new gesture is resisted by the congregation, though the meaning of their resistance is still difficult to determine. So, to repeat my final principle about ritual change: Complex religious ritual systems change in ways that can be guided but not controlled by religious authorities or professionals.

THREE CHANGED PATTERNS

I want next to talk about three changed ritual patterns. The three patterns are gathering for Eucharist, the Eucharistic Prayer and the sign of peace. I will compare the *Missale Romanum* 1570—what we did right up until 1969—and the *Missale Romanum* 1970—what we've been doing for the last thirty years—as a way to uncover what the changing gestures at these three moments is now communicating.

1. Gathering for Eucharist

The *Missale Romanum* 1570 says that the liturgy begins as the priest and assistants approach the altar. The *Missale Romanum* 1970 quotes that instruction verbatim, but it adds a participial phrase: *After the people have assembled,* the liturgy begins as the priest and assisting ministers approach the altar. You might think that's an incredibly tiny addition, but it indicates that the two documents stand a world apart from each other. Let me illustrate that point with several examples.

First, the priest's gathering pattern in the *Missale Romanum* 1570 began with vesting in the sacristy; every single vestment had a prescribed Latin prayer to accompany its placement. Then the priest prepared a host on a paten, which he placed on top of a chalice and then covered with cloths and other material. He picked up this collection of vessels and coverings and held that in his hands to carry to the altar as part of the opening procession.

The assistant ministers—the altar boys—also had a gathering pattern. They too had to go to the sacristy, where they vested but without prescribed texts. Garbed (usually) in cassock and surplice, they checked on wine and water cruets, the lavabo bowl, and a hand towel, but, in fact, since they were usually little kids, they didn't prepare these items—the sacristan prepared them well in advance of Mass. The servers simply checked to make sure they were in place. Then, back in the sacristy, they were to wait in silence until the priest was ready to process from the sacristy to the foot of the altar.

In the 1570 model, the congregation's gathering pattern had them walking through the church door into the nave and stopping to bless themselves from one of the holy-water stoups (bowls or containers) situated at the entryway. Then they moved to an appropriate pew, either one of their own choice, or one to which they were directed by the usher, or, in some eras, one they had rented for their family. Each person genuflected at the entry to the pew, orienting one's body toward the tabernacle positioned at the center of the high altar, and, as a really good Catholic, you knew you went down on one knee when the tabernacle doors were closed and on two knees when the tabernacle doors were open. Once in the pew, most people knelt to make a personal preparation for Mass, then settled back to wait until a bell signaled everyone to rise.

The pattern in the *Missale Romanum* 1970 is a bit different. The priest's gathering pattern begins in the sacristy, where he vests but is not bound to any prescribed Latin prayers (or in any other language, for that matter). The chalice, paten, bread, and appropriate linen cloths are normally not carried in the procession; they're prepared at some other place. He may remain in the sacristy, perhaps sharing prayer with all the ministers, or he may go to the entryway of the church and greet parishioners as they come in.

Now the assistant ministers—formerly only the altar boys—may include a deacon, lector or lectors, acolyte or acolytes, eucharistic ministers, cantor or cantors, and music director: Their gathering pattern varies. Some of them vest, others don't: It's up to the tradition of the local community. None, however, have prescribed prayers for putting on their clothes. Each is responsible for his or her own ministry objects: The deacon checks the Gospel Book; the lector checks the readings and the intercessions; the acolytes check the cross and the candles. There may be shared prayer among them but nothing prescribed, rather something arising from the heart. Those in the opening procession may wait in the sacristy or at the doorway until the procession starts, and those not in the opening procession simply move out into the body of the church where they take their place at their ministerial locales.

What's the congregation's pattern in the 1970 *Ordo*? They stop at a gathering space, which could be a plaza in front of the church or the narthex. They enter the nave, receiving bulletins and worship aids from greeters. They may bless themselves with holy water, but that water may now be found only in a centrally located font, not in containers at each of the doors: The stoups at the doorways have disappeared. They might genuflect or bow or make no gesture before taking their seat (and an usher usually directs them to a seat only if the church is crowded or if they arrive late). Their gestures of reverence may be directed toward the altar, especially if the tabernacle is located in some side chapel. They may kneel or sit for silent prayer, or they may engage in conversation until liturgical ministers rehearse the assembly in song, make announcements, and/or invite the assembly to rise.

Can you see from these examples how radically the gestural patterns of gathering have been transformed in thirty-five years? There's a reason, frankly, why members of our assembly will still resist a rehearsal before Mass: The older members in particular (whose example is very important to younger members) have been trained—and trained very well—at the level of their mammalian brains that what you do when you enter the sacred space is move into silence and quasi-contemplative prayer. Against that rooted pattern they find themselves facing some jerk up in front of the assembly leaning into a microphone and telling them: "You vill sing und you vill enjoy it!" No wonder we've got a problem with reforming our gathering pattern.

2. *The Eucharistic Prayer*

In the *Missale Romanum* 1570, the priest's gestural and postural pattern for the Eucharistic Prayer was facing toward the tabernacle. (Describing this posture as standing "with his back toward the faithful" is prejudicial. The intent was that the priest faced the tabernacle on the highest step of the altar, assuming a position as the leader of a phalanx of worshipers all mutually oriented in the same direction: toward the tabernacle and the back wall of the church.) Facing the tabernacle, the priest extended his hands to give the *"Dominus vobiscum"* greeting, lifted his hands for the *"Sursum corda,"* and brought them into a folded stance for *"Gratias agamus Domino Deo nostro."* (Some older priests still follow this gestural pattern at the beginning of the Eucharistic Prayer—and some younger priests have adopted it as well.) Then the priest moved into the *orans* position, which was strictly controlled by the rubrics and kept the priest's arms in front of his body and below his shoulders, effectively shielding this prayer posture from that phalanx of believers ranked behind him. Until the dialogue Mass was allowed, the servers were the only ones to respond to the priest's spoken invitation to enter the prayer, or, in a *missa cantata*, the choir sang the responses. The rest of the assembly said nothing, and they saw only the priest's back. So, the priest stands in the *orans* position for the preface, and, after he (perhaps with the servers or the choir) recites or chants the *Sanctus* and *Benedictus,* he engages in a complex set of ritual gestures during the *canon Missae,* including multiple hand blessings over the bread and wine: *"Et benedicas haec dona, haec munera, haec sancta sacrificial illibata . . . ."* There was also an extension of hands over the paten and chalice (*"Quam oblationem . . . ."*), accompanied by a bell signal. The priest then engaged in mimetic gestures during the consecration: After looking up as the Latin text evoked the memory of Jesus "looking up to heaven," the priest bent down and addressed the text in a whisper to the elements: "He took bread in his holy and venerable hands, he said the blessing, broke the bread, gave it to his friends, saying, *"Hoc est enim corpus meum"*—and the gesture is very clearly oriented toward the bread. Likewise for the cup. After the consecration he lifted the elements over his head for adoration, accompanied by genuflections before after. From this point on, the priest yoked thumb and forefinger, since they had touched the consecrated elements, even when he stood in the *orans* position. He beat his breast at *"Nobis quoque peccatoribus,"* and he gave a slight lifting of the consecrated cup and bread at the time of the doxology. But he didn't raise them above his head, as at the consecration, nor did he turn around and show the host and chalice to anyone. He was still facing the altar, but now the rest of the assembly finally got to hear part of the prayer spoken or sung aloud: *"Per ipsum, et cum ipso, et in ipso . . . per omnia saecula saeculorum,"* to which the servers, or choir, or, eventually, the whole congregation got to respond "Amen."

The most important observation to make about this entire complex gestural system is that it was largely unseen, except from the back, by the rest of the gathered assembly. It didn't, in fact, illustrate for them any of the ritual texts. It was a sacred choreography aimed primarily at the stance the presider takes: He's assuming the role of Christ as he addresses these words to the Father.

What did the assisting ministers do during the Eucharistic Prayer? They stood from the opening dialogue to the beginning of the *Sanctus*; they knelt for the rest of the prayer. They rang bells at the extension of the priest's hands before the consecration. They also rang bells when he lifted the consecrated elements, and they may have lifted the back of his vestment to allow his arms more freedom to lift the elements higher.

What did the congregation do? They stood from the opening dialogue through the beginning of the *Sanctus*, and then they knelt for the rest of the prayer. They were encouraged to strike their breasts when the bells rang, as a sign of humility, and when the priest struck his at *"Nobis quoque peccatoribus."* If they were choir members, they could remain standing, though that was allowed only if the choir were in the gallery or behind a screen, so they wouldn't be a bad influence on or a distraction to the rest of the assembly. And they remained standing during the singing of the *Sanctus-Benedictus*—which, in its musical settings frankly covered the entire ritual choreography of the canon before and after the consecration. (Our current *Sanctus* acclamation was set, musically, in two parts, so that it would not interrupt the words of institution.) If you were a progressive Catholic, not a member of the choir, you read prayers from your hand missal while you were kneeling, Latin on one side and English on the other. And just so you knew where you were, many hand missals provided little pictures on the side of the page that showed you what it looked like when the priest enacted his assigned gestures (which were otherwise invisible to you). Sometimes the missal indicated when the bells were supposed to ring, so you could know where the priest was in his assigned text—because, of course, you couldn't hear it. If you were slightly less progressive, you read devotional prayers from another book. If you were even less progressive, you prayed a rosary. And if you were the least progressive kind of Catholic, you were just there because you could fulfill your Sunday Mass obligation by attending the offertory, consecration, and priest's Communion. This was the major segment of Mass for which you had to be physically present in order to complete the requirements of Church law.

The details of our current practice at the Eucharistic Prayer should be familiar enough that I need not rehearse them here. But you can understand how radically different the gestural activity is today from the pre-1970 practice. The instant the presidential figure is no longer "facing" God at the head of a phalanx but instead extends his arms to create a circle around the Lord's table, although the texts may not be radically changed, the subtext creates a different world from the one envisioned in the *Missale Romanum* 1570. Again, though the actual words of Eucharistic Prayer I (the Roman Canon) may be no different from those used before 1970, once they are proclaimed aloud and in the vernacular, with the people responding in song throughout the prayer, there is a new world created. Frankly, it's not a surprise that priests who do not know what's going on in a liturgical celebration of the Eucharistic Prayer, as presented by the *Missale Romanum* 1970 feel that it's important for them to alter their stance and actions radically at the words of institution to mime what Jesus did at the Last Supper. It's so much more dramatic, after all, if they bend over the bread, break it, and reach out with the broken halves of the host in direct imitation of the text. "But, Father, we're not here to watch you play Jesus. We're here to have you pray the Eucharistic Prayer in our name as together we make Eucharist around the Lord's table." Understand the issue involved in our current practice: The assigned texts and the gestures for the Eucharist Prayer, especially when exaggerated at the words of institution, are sometimes informing each other, sometimes subverting each other.

3. The Sign of Peace

According to the *Missale Romanum* 1570, the priest, standing at the altar, facing toward the tabernacle, took the broken parts of the host and moved them in a sign of the cross over the chalice, while saying, *"Pax Domini sit semper vobiscum."* (Note that the Latin text has "you" in the plural!) Was this gesture really being addressed to the consecrated elements, as the gesture would indicate? Only if the community were celebrating a *missa solemnis* (solemn high Mass)—only then, and only after he had made the gesture over the chalice, would the priest kiss the altar, turn, and exchange a clerical hug with the deacon. Only with the deacon. Then he would turn back to the altar and continue the preparatory gestures toward Communion.

What would the assisting ministers do? If it were a *missa cantata* or a *missa lecta*—what we used to call high Mass and low Mass, sung Mass or recited Mass—there would be no gesture at all during the response to the *Pax Domini: "Et cum spiritu tuo."* If it were a *missa solemnis* (solemn high Mass), however, the ministers would exchange clerical hugs in hierarchical order: deacon to subdeacon, subdeacon to master of ceremonies, master of ceremonies to second master of ceremonies, second master of ceremonies to the clergy who may be in the sanctuary (including those in "minor orders")—but the sign of peace gesturally ended at the sanctuary rail. The faithful never exchanged it; it was only a clerical act. What, then, did the congregation do? If it were a dialogue Mass, they would actually say the response along with the servers: *"Et cum spiritu tuo."* That's it; they didn't turn to one another and embrace, or shake hands, or anything.

Today, however, the sign of peace is a bit different, even if we still have to figure out a gestural ritual form that can bear the weight of the texts. For example, some will say, as the *General Instruction of the Roman Missal* 2000 directs, that after the priest extends his hands and says, "The peace of the Lord be with you always," and the congregation responds ("And also with you"), then his task is to stay at the altar. He doesn't go down among the faithful. Why does he need to go among them and individually shake hands, since he's already engaged in a verbal and gestural interchange with the entire assembly? Let the assembly, then, share with each other, while the priest exchanges a sign of peace with the ministers in the sanctuary. The gesture doesn't have to start hierarchically from the altar, as the gestures in the older rite indicated, and come gradually moving its way down past the sanctuary rail: Let the entire assembly gesture it.

Our current ritual problem is the gesture. Right now, as we invite the peace of the Lord for our neighbors, we use a gesture borrowed from common Rotarian fellowship—the same gesture, in fact, that people use when they have just concluded a contract and screwed someone else to the wall. That is going to be our gesture of peace? The alternative to a Rotarian handshake seems to be the "liturgical press": hug, hug, hug, hug, hug. In that case, the gesture that is supposed to establish unity among the assembly becomes so intrusive that significant portions of the assembly back away from it. (My all-time favorite is the sign of peace at daily Mass: a wave or even the peace sign offered across the ten pews that separate everyone, and, when we can get to it at Communion or after Mass, the exchange of the ritual text: "The peace of the Lord be always with you.") Pastoral musicians, unfortunately, sometimes add to the problem of developing an appropriate gesture for the sign of peace. Recognizing that the ritual text and the gestural repertoire are in absolute chaos, they decide to sing a peace song because everyone can at least sing together: "Let there be peace on earth." Then "progressive" composers decide to take the "Lamb of God" and the peace song and put them on top of each other. The problem with this ritual action, as with all rituals in which people don't know what they're doing, is that ritual abhors a vacuum. If the gesture or its intent is not clear, then the entire thing is going to flower in all sorts of directions, which then calls for later discernment on the part of trained communities in order to calm things down, do some pruning, clarify the ritual action.

TRANSFORMED BY THE LITURGY

I want to suggest to those who think that there are major things going on simply because of the change in music—a change from a sacred language to a vernacular, a change from vernaculars to multiple registers of a vernacular, a change from a single vernacular to multiple vernaculars—to those who think that such changes have transformed us, I suggest that the ritual patterns underlying those spoken and sung texts have changed us even more. First, they've changed our understanding of God. This is very hard to deal with. If there is a zone of contestation about how the liturgy has transformed our understanding on this matter, it's partially over where God is going to be situated in a postmodern world. The coherence of the *Missale Romanum* 1570 on this point was clear: You knew where God was situated, and you knew your place vis-à-vis God. It was clear then; it is not so clear now. The zone of contestation in our rituals about where is God situated in the midst of this worshiping assembly is tearing our communities apart. I honestly think that is not going to be solved by executive fiat but by

66

communities' doing some very deep discernment work about how we cling to the transcendence of God but to the transcendence of a God who chose to enter imminently into our life experience. What do we do? How do we ritualize that understanding?

Second, the shift in ritual has transformed the experience of Christ. I believe the shift has been from a ritualization of Christ as magically transformed and inhering in hosts and wine and water to an understanding of multiple presences of Christ in the assembly: a presence in the preached word, in the proclaimed word, in the person of the multiple ministers, and in the assembly itself when it sings and prays. We have moved from a simple identification of Christic presence in the consecrated elements into a very complex, multiple mode of presencing, and, frankly our theology has barely begun to try to catch up with that shift. We have some wonderful theology that was set up for an earlier understanding of Christic presence devolving on the elements; we do not have a sophisticated theology for the multiple presences of Christ in the worshiping assembly.

Third, liturgy has transformed our experience and understanding of the Holy Spirit. I don't want to overstate this, but it would be fairly safe to say that, in its eucharistic forms, the *Missale Romanum* 1570 almost totally ignored the Holy Spirit. This absence was not an explicit mode of discourse, song, or gesture; it was more of an oversight. During the post-Vatican II reform, we got to restore at least a little bit of the recognition of the Spirit's activity, but that restoration is just in its infancy. We barely have texts about it, and we certainly don't have gestures about it beyond the imposition of hands.

Liturgy has also transformed our experience and understanding of the Church. If you were a Catholic forty years ago, you would have believed, first, that the Church equals Roman Catholicism, or, for most people in the United States, the Latin Rite of Roman Catholicism. (Oh, sure, there were those odd Eastern Rite Churches, but we didn't worry much about them.) So, within Roman Catholicism, the Church existed in three categories: the Church triumphant, namely all the angels and saints; the Church militant—think about that as a fundamental image—namely, those living in this world of space and time; and the Church suffering, the Church in purgatory.

I don't think honestly that those categories would be the categories that average people in the pew would use today if we asked them what the Church is. They might possibly talk about discipleship; they're certainly going to talk about Jesus. Have we developed adequate categories to talk about the mystery of the Church? No, but we are clear that the former division into triumphant, militant, and suffering is not adequate. The struggle we're facing in naming and describing the Church includes the problem we have once we've got a eucharistic table and a presider gathering an assembly around the Lord's table, and it becomes increasingly difficult to fence access to the table off from anyone who wishes to come. Forty years ago, two-thirds of the people at Sunday Mass might not receive Communion, but they were present for Mass. If your parish today is anything like mine, nearly everyone comes to Communion. If you're not going to come to Communion, you don't come to the ritual. And here is where the zone of contestation lies: How dare we baptize some folks, recognize their baptism, and then fence them off from the Lord's table! How different—and difficult—the questions are becoming.

Transformations caused by our ritual behavior are also occurring in our experience and understanding of clergy and laity. Forty years ago our categories were simple. The Church had two big divisions: There was the clerical division, which had the tasks of teaching, governing, and sanctifying, and there were the laity: those who were taught, governed, and sanctified. That easy division disappears when one reads *Gaudium et spes* and *Lumen gentium*. In those conciliar documents about the Church in its nature and in its pastoral work, the tasks of teaching (or, better, proclaiming), governing, transforming the structures of the world, sanctifying, and entering into God's own holiness devolve on the Church as a whole. Clergy and laity have mutual responsibilities for those shared tasks. Have we begun to see that insight into ecclesial identity ritualized in our gestural and postural forms at liturgy?

Finally, there are the transformations of our experience and understanding of the created order. I would be willing to suspect that most folks forty years ago, if asked to articulate their hope, would express it as leaving behind this "vale of tears," so that after the present suffering we might enter into the glory that's been prepared for us. I don't deny that yearning: The "vale of tears" is still a quite accurate description of life for many of us, if not for all of us. But I think the understanding of the created order has shifted: It is now seen not just as something dangerous against which we must keep ourselves pure but, rather, it has becomes the medium—the mode—for sacramental encounter with God. To make this transformation concrete: We are not druids, we are not nature worshipers; we don't offer grapes and wheat as our sacrifice to God: we don't offer nature raw. What we do is offer bread and wine to be transformed by the Spirit. Bread and wine are co-creations between God, who gives us wheat and grapes, and humanity, whose reptilian, mammalian, and neocortical brain has been able to steward and transform grapes and wheat into wine and bread. It's the bread and wine, formed by our shaping of God's creation, that is then transformed under the power of prayer, not simply grapes and wheat. That insight gives us a theology of ecology; it also gives us a sense that, although we have no lasting city here in this world of space and time, it's still our home. It's still something God has given us.

Fr. Jan Michael Joncas, a presbyter of the Roman Catholic Archdiocese of St. Paul–Minneapolis, Minnesota, serves as associate professor of Catholic studies and theology at the University of St. Thomas, St. Paul, Minnesota. He holds degrees in liturgical studies from the University of Notre Dame and the Pontifical Liturgical Institute at S. Anselmo in Rome. He is the author of three books, numerous articles, and seventeen collections of liturgical music.

5

Being Beautiful, Being Just

Nathan D. Mitchell

I feel privileged to be giving this lecture as part of a series that honors
Fr. Robert Hovda, that dear and glorious curmudgeon who refused, as
Don Saliers once said, to squander the gifts God had so liberally be-
stowed on him—gifts of "high intelligence, gracious pen, ironic wit,
deft persuasion through speech—all put to use in serving two relent-
less taskmasters, integrity and truth."[1] Many of you may remember
Bob's challenging presence at NPM conventions. Perhaps you can still
hear, as I do, his broken, raspy voice that faded in and out like those
early radios built on vacuum-tube technology. Perhaps you recall his
passion, his mordant humor, his fierce conviction that "our rock-bot-
tom human and baptismal unity is what makes church," that "our
coming together to realize church before the one All-holy [God], our
being in one place at one time for one common prayer-action . . . is
what Sunday Mass is all about."[2]

Bob was a prophet intensely aware (as Jeremiah was) of what happens to whistle-blowers who preach truth to power. In short, Bob
Hovda was a healer who made no bones about his own fragility, his
vulnerability, his hunger for healing, for serenity and sobriety, for truth-
fulness and integrity. And yes, for beauty. Better than most, Bob knew
that to be made in God's image is to be created in beauty, but he recognized, ruefully, how often we stray, stumble and "fall short of the glory
of God." Still, it was that divine glory that Bob served—doggedly,
painfully, yet gladly, until he drew his last breath on February 5, 1992.

---

[1] Don Saliers, "The Berakah Award for 1982" (honoring Robert W. Hovda), in
John Baldovin, ed., *Robert Hovda: The Amen Corner* (Collegeville: The Liturgical
Press, Pueblo Books, 1994) 254.

[2] Robert Hovda, "So Knit Thou Our Friendship Up," in Baldovin, ed., *Robert
Hovda: The Amen Corner*, 94.

My theme is "on beauty and being just," a phrase derived from the title of a short but important book published by Elaine Scarry in 1999.[3] Dr. Scarry is the Walter M. Cabot Professor of Aesthetics and the General Theory of Value at Harvard University, so she is well qualified to comment on the relation between ethics and aesthetics, justice and beauty, the life of virtue and the life of art. It is her conviction that in real life, ideas like "fairness" and "justice" tend to be—or become—abstract. That is precisely where beauty's work begins. Beautiful objects, sounds, visions, and persons do not merely excite our senses and arouse our imaginations; they stop us dead in our tracks, they transfix us, filling us with what Scarry calls a "surfeit of aliveness." Beauty thus draws us away—if only for a moment—from the self's persistent preoccupation with its own feelings, ambitions, goals, and agenda; it forces us to focus on *the other*, on *others*, on a center that exists *outside* our cheap selves. That is why art always acts as an antidote against self-absorption, self-centeredness. Beauty takes the center *out of* self and places it elsewhere by demanding that we reckon with it, come to terms with it. That is art's saving grace.

So in the first part of my presentation, I want to outline some of Professor Scarry's ideas about beauty because they lay a firm foundation for exploring the relation between aesthetics and ethics, art and justice. My brief outline will consist of four points about beauty:

1) Beauty first comes to us as a greeting, a salutation, a summons: a call that invites response, provokes reaction. Beauty is those two dramatic, *sforzando* E-flat-major chords that raise the curtain on Beethoven's "Eroica" symphony; it's that almost deafening crash of catgut, brass, woodwinds, and voices shouting "Behold the sea!" that launches Ralph Vaughan Williams's first symphony; it's a world so "charged with the grandeur of God" that it flames out "like shining from shook foil";[4] it's an archangel with fiery face and rainbow wings rushing toward an obscure Palestinian village to meet a young woman who's unwed, pregnant, and clueless. In all these, *beauty* greets *us—it* beckons *us* to be, to dwell, in *its* presence. Beauty is less about seeing than about being seen, less about hearing than about being heard. As Scarry puts it, our arrival at beauty's door "seems contractural, not

[3] Elaine Scarry, *On Beauty and Being Just* (Princeton, N.J.: Princeton University Press, 1999).

[4] Phrases from Gerard Manley Hopkins's poem, "God's Grandeur."

just something *you* want, but something the world you are now join-ing wants."[5]

Standing on beauty's threshold, however, we recognize that *beauty* is calling the shots, that *it* has summoned *us*—not vice versa. This is exactly what the German poet Rainer Maria Rilke tells us he felt when he first gazed at an ancient sculpture of Apollo (perhaps the magnifi-cent Belvedere Apollo): He was not looking at the statue; rather, the statue, with its torso "glistening like a wild beast's fur," was looking at him. In its presence Rilke concludes, "there is no place / that does not see you. You must change your life."[6] *You must change your life!* As Rilke puts it in another poem, "God" is the dreamer, and "I" am what God dreams.[7] What the poet says of God can be said of the beautiful: it is like some ancient tower that you can circle for ten thousand years and still never know whether you're "a falcon, a storm, / or an unfin-ished song."[8]

Beauty is thus a greeting, a welcome, a summons, a call to conver-sion: *you must change your life.*

2) Beauty is characterized by three features that are fairly familiar and a fourth that is equally important but a bit more difficult to grasp. First, the three familiar features: to experience beauty is to experience something (a) sacred, (b) unprecedented, and (c) life-saving. In the presence of the beautiful, the hard line between the divine and the human, the sacred and the secular, almost vanishes. We can hear this happening on the very first pages of the book of Genesis. God shows all of Eden's creatures to Adam and suggests that he choose a partner from among them (2:18-20). Apparently Adam gets cranky and balks, so God relents and, following a night of creative anatomy, produces something new: a woman. Adam's response is immediate and over-whelming, "At last," he cries in the Bible's most ancient poem, "at last! This one is bone of my bones and flesh of my flesh! She is to be called Woman because she was taken from Man!" (2:23).

Notice what happens. What fills the scene isn't the praise of God but human rejoicing. If Adam had been a properly obedient and

---

[5] Scarry, *On Beauty and Being Just*, 26; emphasis added.

[6] "Archaic Torso of Apollo," in Stephen Mitchell, trans., *Ahead of All Parting: The Selected Poetry and Prose of Rainer Maria Rilke* (New York: The Modern Library, 1995) 67.

[7] Rilke, untitled poem from "The Book of Hours," in Mitchell, *Ahead of All Parting,* 7.

[8] Ibid., 5.

grateful creature, he would *first* have praised the Creator's ingenuity, thanked God, and only then mentioned his glee at the sight of his new wife. But that's not what Adam does; instead, he reacts to the woman's beauty by making a poem that knocks down the walls between sacred and secular by celebrating the presence of the Holy in the human. Both God's act and Adam's are unprecedented, and the result is life-giving. The two humans cleave to one another as a couple; they "become one flesh," and though both are naked, they feel absolutely no shame—they have nothing to hide, no deadly secrets to conceal.

This brief passage from Genesis reminds us of beauty's familiar features: it is (a) sacred; it is (b) unprecedented; and it is (c) life-giving. But the story also reveals beauty's fourth feature, more difficult and more obscure. That feature, oddly enough, is failure, error. Indeed, Scarry calls the first part of her book "On Beauty and Being *Wrong*." Beauty shows us not only the holy, the unprecedented, and the life-giving; it also reveals our almost limitless human capacity for error and deception, for "getting it wrong," for making mistakes. That's precisely what happens in the book of Genesis. Adam's cry in 2:23 ("This one is flesh of my flesh, bone of my bones") is ecstatic but flawed. For ultimately, the woman is beautiful—she's a sacred, unprecedented, life-giving revelation—not because she's Adam's flesh and bone but because she is *God's* gift. This woman, this source of life and goodness, this "mother of all the living," comes from the Creator's hand rather than from human engineering. Why? Because *all* existence flows from the God who, like a potter, scoops soil from the ground, blows the breath of life into it, and makes earth creatures into living beings (see 2:7). Ironically, it is the sight of Eve's beauty that reveals Adam's error. In a sense, Adam looked at the woman but saw *himself* reflected. What he *should* have seen was an *other*, an other-ness; what he should have seen was God's limitless, life-giving creativity. The woman's beauty channels God's gracious presence, not Adam's preoccupied selfhood.

It's a paradox, isn't it? One of beauty's greatest mercies is its capacity to show us that we are wrong, in error, mistaken, sometimes comically, sometimes tragically. That is why our reaction to the beautiful is so often bewilderment, confusion, or astonishment. As Rilke put it in his sonnet on the ancient torso of Apollo, what we perceive as beautiful seems to glow from within, from a secret country so dazzling that it bursts like a star from all its borders—"for here, there is no place /

that does not see you. You must change your life."⁹ *You must change your life*. Faced with Eve's beauty, Adam discovered that he was wrong—not because he loved his wife but because he failed to see that beauty effaces the self and opens a window on *God*. Nor was Adam alone in his error. The great Greek hero Odysseus makes a similar mistake in Book 6 of Homer's epic, the *Odyssey*.¹⁰ The war-weary, storm-tossed Odysseus meets the lovely Nausicaa (*Naw-sí-kay-a*), daughter of King Alcinous of Phaeacia (*Fee-aý-sha*); he's so impressed that he instantly composes a hymn to her beauty. "I'm at your mercy, princess," he stammers; "just look at you!"

". . . just look
at your build, your bearing, your lithe flowing grace . . .
such a bloom of beauty . . .
I have never laid eyes on anyone like you,
neither man nor woman . . .
I look at you and a sense of wonder takes me."¹¹

(That last line reads, in a more literal translation of Homer's Greek: "Awe has me in its grip as I gaze [at you].") Suddenly, in the midst of this peerless panegyric to Nausicaa's beauty, Odysseus remembers something. "But wait," he cries, "I *did* see something comparable to your beauty once upon a time—it was at Apollo's altar in Delos. There, I saw

"the young slip of a palm-tree springing into the light.
There I'd sailed, you see, with a great army in my wake,
out on the long campaign that doomed my life to hardship.
That vision! Just as I stood there gazing, rapt, for hours . . .
no shaft like that had ever risen up from the earth—
so now I marvel at *you*, my lady: rapt, enthralled,
too struck with awe to grasp you by the knees
though pain has ground me down."¹²

Wrapped in wonder, Odysseus suddenly realized he was wrong. He becomes conscious of his capacity for error. As Scarry explains, Odysseus is so incapacitated by Nausicaa's beauty that "he temporarily forgets the palm by the altar, injuring it by his thoughtless

---

⁹ Rilke, "Archaic Torso of Apollo," in Mitchell, *Ahead of All Parting*, 67.

¹⁰ See discussion in Scarry, *On Beauty and Being Just*, 21–33.

¹¹ Robert Fagles, translator, *Homer: The Odyssey* (New York: Viking, 1996) 173 (= Book 6, lines 166–177, passim).

¹² Ibid. (= Book 6, lines 178–186).

disregard and requiring him at once to go on to correct himself."[13] This experience of being wrong, in error, seems to belong, almost by definition, to the perception of beauty. *You must change your life.*

3) Beauty is never abstract or "general"; it is always about particular things. Someone once said that the business of poetry is to have business with the grass. Poetry is a stubbornly concrete art; it recognizes that the simplest sight—the "young slip of a palm-tree springing into light," the sound of a barking dog—can suddenly propel us toward mystery and holiness. In a poem called "Angels," for example, Irish poet R. T. Smith describes swallows swirling high in an April barn, "worshiping / dry straw, the gold motes / ascending, so many / dusty wings."[14] When he speaks about "milk cooling like moonlight / in brimful tins," I'm carried back to a childhood vision of my dad milking a couple of Guernseys by hand and pouring the steaming white foam into a strainer set atop a gunmetal can. With my own tin cup, I'd scoop up the rich, creamy concoction—still hot from the animal that gave it; I'd lift the cup and drink, letting the cream roll on my tongue, a river of earthly delight.

Beauty is concrete. But more than that, beauty is motion, activity, relationship. Sometimes we talk as though beauty were a "thing," a purchasable commodity. Yet beauty cannot be commodified (though you'd never learn that from contemplating the multibillion-dollar-a-year cosmetic industry). In fact, despite its concreteness, beauty is not a "thing" at all. It's movement, activity, relationship. Beauty doesn't "cling" to people and things the way plastic wrap or dysfunctional codependents do. When we enter the presence of the beautiful, an exchange occurs: one that redefines us.

Perhaps you've experienced something like that during the liturgy. Let's say it's the Easter Vigil, and the community has just welcomed a dozen newly initiated Christians at the Lord's table. The Mass ends, with everyone singing, "Thanks be to God, alleluia, alleluia," and the organist introduces the familiar concluding hymn, "Jesus Christ Is Risen Today." You've sung it a million times before, but suddenly, at that moment, everything comes together: your faith in Christ, your in-

[13] Scarry, *On Beauty and Being Just*, 28. "The hymn to Nausicaa's beauty," Scarry continues, "can instead be called a palinode to the beauty of the palm. By either account, Odysseus starts by making an error."

[14] "Angels," in R. T. Smith, *Trespasser* (Baton Rouge: Louisiana State University Press, 1996) 39.

volvement with the adult initiation process and the newly baptized, the day, the hour, the place, your family. It all comes together—beautifully—and the exchange between you and those events *changes you*. You enter a new relationship with what is, with what is real, with what is beautiful.

Beauty, then, is a beginning, not an ending; a call, not a conclusion; a relationship, not a relic; an action, not an object; a verb, not a noun. That's why Elaine Scarry speaks of "the forward momentum of beautiful things."[15]

4) That leads to the fourth (and final) point in this outline that forms the first part of my presentation. As Elaine Scarry says, beauty has "forward momentum." Our experience of the beautiful incites "the desire to bring new things into the world: infants, epics, sonnets, drawings, dances, laws, philosophic dialogues, theological tracts."[16] To put it another way, beauty bestows on its beholders an unceasing desire to replicate. *Pulchrum est diffusivum sui*[17]—beauty always seeks to extend itself, to prolong the experience, to deepen the desire. In short, beauty begets an unceasing flow of persons, poems, plays, paintings, photos, ploys, plots, and prayers. And the proof of this, Professor Scarry explains, comes from the simple, everyday fact of *staring*. When we see a soaring finch flash golden across the summer sky, our first impulse is not to capture the image in a poem, a play, or a prayer *but simply to keep on staring; we want to prolong the moment*, to keep looking at that finch five seconds longer, fifteen seconds longer, thirty seconds longer—"as long as the bird is there to be beheld."[18] (If you have a teenage daughter, watch her eyes as she witnesses the Backstreet Boys leaving the stage after their concert.)

Why do we stare? Because beauty stirs up in us an insatiable desire *to keep on seeing*, to behold and be held. For we know in some deep corner of our minds that we become what we see—and so our hearts hunger for nothing less that the beautiful vision of God.

My four points about beauty, then, are: (1) it comes to us as a greeting, a salutation, a summons, a call to conversion; (2) it brings us into the presence of the sacred, the unprecedented, the life-saving but, at

[15] Scarry, *On Beauty and Being Just*, 46.

[16] Ibid.

[17] "Beauty diffuses itself;" cf. Thomas Aquinas's comment about goodness: "*Bonum est diffusivum sui esse*," goodness spreads itself around, spreads its very being around. *Summa Theologiae*, Prima Pars, Q. 5. art. 4, corpus.

[18] Scarry, *On Beauty and Being Just*, 6.

the same time, exposes our capacity to be wrong, to be in error, to make mistakes; (3) it is concrete, particular; it has "forward momentum" because beauty is action, motion, relationship rather than commodity, object, or "thing"; and (4) it bestows on the beholder the desire to replicate, to extend the experience, to prolong the moment.

BEING JUST

This part of my presentation explores the connection between beauty and justice, ethics and aesthetics, as these shape our experience of the Church's liturgy.

In part one, I tried to show through examples from the creation story in Genesis and from Book Six of Homer's *Odyssey*, how our experience of beauty as sacred, unprecedented, and life-giving also exposes our liability for error, for being wrong, for making mistakes. Our vulnerability to error provides the crucial link, I think, between beauty and justice. Not only do we fail, often, to credit the proper *source* of beauty, God; we also tend to scorn persons, places, and things that we once regarded as "beautiful" but that now we reject as trivial, amateurish, cheap, kitschy, outdated, or "damaged goods."

Some of us probably thought the song "If I Had a Hammer" was beautiful when Peter, Paul, and Mary sang it forty-odd years ago; we thought it was exactly the right music for those "coffee-table Masses" we flocked to during the mid-1960s. Today, such memories embarrass us; not even geriatric nostalgia can breathe new life into the "'60s folk idiom." We're especially chagrined that we sang such things at Mass! All this is understandable; I'm certainly not recommending a return to that song and the "folk idiom" as suitable music at Masses that focus on "social justice."

Yet our newfound liturgical sophistication (Poulenc motets instead of Peter, Paul, and Mary) may also miss the point. The folk music of the last century was, after all, legitimate art—not "high art," perhaps, not art to be memorialized in museums (not even in the Rock-and-Roll Hall of Fame), certainly not art to be imitated by today's church-music composers, but *art* nonetheless.

One of the strange things about beauty is its inexhaustibility, its plenitude, its surprising capacity to survive. The beautiful is astonishingly agile, plastic, elastic, nimble, capable of continuing to "carry greetings from other worlds even after those worlds have long vanished."[19] So as Elaine Scarry notes, "The temptation to scorn the inno-

[19] Ibid., 47.

cent object for ceasing to be beautiful might be called the temptation against plenitude; it puts at risk not the repudiated object but the capaciousness of the cognitive act."[20] The temptation against plenitude, the refusal to let our minds and imaginations remain "capacious," large-hearted, roomy: those are serious flaws. After all, when we repudiate something formerly experienced as beautiful, it is *we*—and not those objects—who are diminished. So the question we need to ask is: If the face or the figure or the tune we found ravishing for two years seems, in the third, boring, bland, and unappealing—who has changed?

Who has changed? That's the question. Beauty not only confronts us with unprecedented joy and pleasure; it also convicts us of error and fickleness. That brings me back to my theme of justice. At the end of Book One in her best-selling novel *Death in Holy Orders*, P. D. James summarizes a homily given at St. Anselm's theological college by Archdeacon Crampton (who is later murdered). The archdeacon's theme was Christian discipleship in the modern world, and his message was unambiguous:

Modern discipleship [Crampton urged] was not a matter of indulgence in archaic if beautiful language, in which words more often obscured than affirmed the reality of faith. There was a temptation to over-value intelligence and intellectual achievement so that theology became a philosophical exercise in justifying skepticism. Equally seductive was an over-emphasis on ceremony, vestments, and disputed points of procedure, an obsession with competitive musical excellence, which too often transformed a church service into a public performance. The Church was not a social organization with which the comfortable middle class could satisfy its craving for beauty, order, nostalgia, and the illusion of spirituality. Only by a return to the truth of the Gospel could the Church hope to meet the needs of the modern world.[21]

Sound familiar? James's fictional archdeacon has a point, I think. It is very easy to confuse our desire for decorum and "beauty in worship" with nostalgia, self-indulgence, snobbish appeals to "artistic excellence," the costly amusements of the rich and privileged, pandering to wealthy "art patrons," and, most fatally, the assumption that God loves the poor but hates their art. I'm not making a manifesto here for

---

[20] Ibid., 49–50.
[21] P. D. James, *Death in Holy Orders* (New York: Alfred A. Knopf, 2001) 146.

the inclusion of inferior art in Catholic worship. On the contrary, we must work with all the talent and energy we can muster to see that what the Sunday assembly sings is both good ritual music and good art. That's why, for example, I'd reject the use of Mozart and Haydn Masses in modern Catholic worship: they're good art, indeed great art, but they're not "good ritual music." By the same token, some of the chant settings in the present Roman *Sacramentary* (as well as some contemporary settings of the Eucharistic Prayer) strike me as neither great art nor good ritual music. They're clumsy, insipid, and difficult for either presiders or congregations to sing. In a word, there's plenty of room for improvement.

But what does all this have to do with our theme, "beauty and justice"? Well, *everything*. I've repeated a line from Rilke's sonnet on the ancient torso of Apollo several times: *"You must change your life."* I've spent time, too, speaking about Elaine Scarry's insight that our experience of beauty reveals our capacity for error, for being wrong. At this critical stage in the evolution of the postconciliar liturgical renewal, I think it's time for repentance and new priorities. Perhaps that sounds odd, but I think it's our only way forward. In one of his very first "Amen Corner" columns, Bob Hovda wrote these prophetic words:

"There is a devil abroad whose ascendancy is especially tempting, and whose masquerade obstructs and diminishes certain essential aspects of church reform and renewal in many of the quarters where serious efforts are happily occurring. It is a devil that pretends to be the friend of the poor and oppressed, but it identifies the faith community's need of festivity's 'excess,' of beauty and artistry in the environments and other elements of celebration, as the enemy of social justice."[22]

In other words, "concern for the poor" does not excuse the slovenly, inattentive, and downright ugly things priests and people sometimes do at Sunday Mass. Hovda goes on to explain that the poor themselves have a much better sense of what "festivity" and "excess" are all about than jaded rich people from the suburbs. Wrote Hovda:

"Oppressed and dispossessed people seem to understand the human need for festivity's 'conscious excess' better than affluent or comfortable ones. A party, a festivity, a celebration, a liturgy, has, for people who live daily with the aching pain of want, a psychological and so-

[22] "Scripture Has It, Not on Bread Alone Shall Human Creatures Live," in Baldovin, ed., *Robert Hovda: The Amen Corner*, 161.

cial function whose healing power those who do not so live can scarcely imagine. Glimpses of this truth are everywhere, if we open our eyes. When, for example, a committee was planning an ethnic day for black people (many of them poor and all of them oppressed) before the Philadelphia Eucharistic Congress several years ago, a black representative to the committee laughed uproariously at their middle-class concern that the vesture of the participating bishops should not be, in any way, excessive. The black priest, who had lived with American racist oppression every day of his life, thought their concern very, very funny, and said, 'If any one of those bishops were felt by the people to be *our own*, really with us and belonging to us, the more excessive the festivity and the more impressive the vesture, the better! Without that feeling, even their presence is an affront.'"[23]

And let the Church say, "Amen!" Bob went on to comment that it isn't our "commitment to the gospel that has made us contemptuous of beauty, art, and that reverence for things, materials, forms, that open us to the language of being. It is rather the diminishment of a culture which has domesticated our gospel and robbed us of our power to serve it."[24] Amen, amen. I mean, when politicians in the United States House and Senate (and sadly, when politicians sitting on the Supreme Court, masquerading as judges) start promoting themselves as Christian ethicists and theologians and (worse!) start spouting the Bible, you know we are in trouble—deep, *deep* trouble. There probably aren't enough ethics on Capitol Hill to be detected even with the aid of a particle accelerator.

The solution to poverty isn't ugly art and sappy music in our worship. On the contrary, "the more striking [the] beauty and integrity and careful celebration"[25] of the Sunday liturgy, the deeper "Rilke's rule" sinks in: *You must change your life. We* must change our lives—*together*. The solution to hunger, homelessness, oppression, racism, homophobia, and the host of other social evils that destroy lives isn't careless liturgy, it's repentance, it's *changing our lives*; it's the voluntary renunciation of those addictions—to power, money, and control—that continue to divide the world into "haves" and "have-nots." We won't feed the world's hungry by neglecting the liturgy.

[23] Ibid., 168.
[24] Ibid., 168–69.
[25] Ibid., 169.

But I digress. I want to propose to you a set of four "new priorities" that I believe might help us to create a more just world and, at the same time, to celebrate more beautiful liturgy.

New priority # 1: **Find out. Get informed.** If we want liturgies that are both beautiful and just, we have to quit "guessing" what the poor need or want. For some of us, "finding out" may be easier than you think: you might be surprised to learn how many people, even in affluent suburban parishes, are barely "getting by" (single moms, people with AIDS, elders on fixed incomes who rely on bus trips to Canada for the drugs they desperately need and can ill afford). If you have access to the Internet, log on to www.thehungersite.com, and with one click of your mouse (at no cost to you), you can give a cup of food each day to the hungry. You'll find out how many people on our planet die each day of starvation (24,000; that's 161,000 each week and 8,760,000 each year—a planetary holocaust caused by hunger). You'll also find out where and how to shop at businesses that support food and nutrition programs for the poor.

Or if you have qualms about supporting "secular" organizations, log on to www.focushope.edu. There, you'll get acquainted with Mrs. Eleanor M. Josaitis, a Catholic laywoman (married, mother of five kids), who's been at work since the Detroit race riots of 1967 to increase awareness of hunger and malnutrition, to formulate public policy that supports responsible anti-poverty legislation, and to provide fast-track education (through facilities like Focus Hope's Center for Advanced Technologies) that leads to good jobs in high-tech industries. (Incidentally, when Mrs. Josaitis first began her work, her own mother hired a lawyer to get her daughter declared an "unfit parent." Mom eventually changed her mind!)

Or if you prefer something on the East Coast, log on to www.newcommunity.org to find out more about Msgr. William Linder's work among the poor of Newark's Central Ward. Thirty-five years ago, the Central Ward was so sunk in urban blight that it seemed unredeemable. Today, that area of Newark has emerged as a lively community with sound, attractive housing for low-income residents, with banks and parks and supermarkets and schools that supply access and opportunity where formerly there was nothing but chaos, disorder, and despair.

Or if you live in the Washington, D.C., area, take a short trip some Sunday morning to Bristow, Virginia, and worship with the Benedictine sisters there. These courageous women not only educate children at their excellent schools (Linton Hall in Bristow, St. Gertrude's in Richmond), they also run a program called B.A.R.N. ("Benedictines in Aid and Relief to Neighbors"), which accepts about twenty poor, single mothers (and their children), provides them clean, attractive apartments on the monastery grounds, and places them in a two-year residential program where they learn all the skills needed to function successfully at home, in society, and in the workplace. These women leave the B.A.R.N. program with dignity, a driver's license, their own transportation, a job, and money in the bank. (Incidentally, you'll find that these Benedictine women not only know about justice, they also know how to worship with dignity, style, and grace. Their former prioress is a first-rate pastoral musician.)

So there's no excuse. Information is available. *Priority # 1: Find out. Get informed.*

New priority # 2: **Do something. Get involved**. The curse of poverty isn't merely lack of resources; it's lack of significance. To be poor is to be erased, expendable, negligible, invisible. So the poor don't need our lamentation and hand wringing; they need visibility, action, access, opportunity, jobs, cash. We sometimes forget that when Jesus told the story about "the widow's mite," he was not indulging some Louisa May Alcott fantasy about "how fun it is to be poor." Unfortunately, those of us who live privileged lives routinely misinterpret Jesus' words. We think he is praising that poor widow woman's generosity, whereas in fact he's rejecting and satirizing a religious and economic system that taxed the destitute in order to "support and enhance" the Temple liturgy. The widow, Jesus implies, should have *kept* her money! She, after all, had more right to be called God's temple than any structure built of blood, sweat, and stone.

Still, even people of modest means can perhaps walk to the public library, log on to "the hunger site," and donate a cup of food. After all, to somebody starving, that cup of rice can mean the difference, literally, between life and death. Because that, you see, is our problem: we no longer grasp the difference between life and death. We're creating a culture where consumption trumps compassion, where voyeurism replaces vision, where death is so expensive the poor can't afford it and life is so deadly the rich can't stand it. We've created a culture where "having it all" leads to such crashing boredom that our young go berserk and shoot up their high-school classmates. There's a problem here, a problem we have to start facing: we must first find out how to *stop* feeding *that* culture, and *start* feeding those who are victims of it.

Granted, there's no magic bullet, no "one size fits all" solution to neediness. Perhaps you should sell your gas-guzzling SUV (to reduce consumption of fossil fuels)—or perhaps *not* (less auto production means fewer jobs). There are no facile solutions, no easy answers. The point is not to find an action plan everybody can agree on (this will never happen); *the point is for each of us to find a plan we can act on*. Some of us may be able to tithe our time (delivering meals on wheels, for instance); others of us may tithe our money. If you can tithe neither time nor money, tithe your heart: Give it away in love and prayer. The point is to do *something* rather than nothing.

Pope John Paul II has often referred to the "fundamental option for the poor," a phrase that originated among liberation theologians in Latin America. Of course the word "option" is misleading because there really isn't anything "optional" about it. Christians have an *obligation* to help the poor, actively and specifically. St. John Chrysostom was very blunt about it: "Not to enable the poor to share in our goods is to steal from them," he said in a homily on the rich man and Lazarus, "[it is to] deprive them of life. The goods we possess are not ours, but theirs."[26] That's a pretty blunt moral mandate, quoted, of all places, in the *Catechism of the Catholic Church*. In fact, the *Catechism* (# 1397) explicitly links our participation in the Eucharist with commitment to the poor: "To receive in truth the Body and Blood of Christ given up for us, we must recognize Christ in the poorest, his brethren." The *Catechism* then goes on to cite another homily of John Chrysostom, which declares "You dishonor this table when you do not judge worthy of sharing your food someone judged worthy to take part in this meal."[27]

Words like that don't give us much wiggle room, ethically; their meaning is sharp, clear, and obvious. We have no choice but to help the poor because, as the seventeenth-century French bishop Jacques-Benigne Bossuet once said, the Church permits rich folk to become members *only on condition that they serve the poor*.[28] Imagine what a

[26] See the *Catechism of the Catholic Church* (New York: Paulist Press, 1994) # 2446. The reference is to a homily by St. John Chrysostom *de Lazaro* 2.5 (Greek text in J. P. Migne, ed., *Patrologia Graeca* [PG] [Paris, 1857–1866] 48: 992).

[27] The reference is to Chrysostom's homily on 1 Corinthians 27.4 (Greek text in PG 61: 229–30).

[28] See Bossuet's homily on "The Great Dignity of the Poor," preached on Septuagesima Sunday; French text of the sermon in *Oeuvres complètes de Bossuet* (12 vols.; Besancon: Outhenin-Chalandre Fils, 1836) vol. 1, 187–93.

transformation might occur if we took these episcopal exhortations by Chrysostom and Bossuet seriously. It's astonishing to think that we Catholics often punish politicians who support abortion, yet we applaud the "fiscal responsibility and discipline" of politicians who refuse to vote a dime to relieve hunger, hardship, and homelessness. I've often wondered what might happen if, instead of complaining about "liturgical abuses" or "unorthodox opinions" among clergy and people, our bishops were to begin placing under interdict those parishes and dioceses that refused—in specific, concrete, and accountable ways—to share their resources with the hungry.

New priority # 3: **Look around. Pay attention.** If we are to do the work of justice, we need an understanding of beauty in the liturgy that includes and embraces *imperfection*. I once read an article whose author used the phrase "Glory to God in the *lowest!*" He was chiding those who believe that "beauty in art" is to be identified with social status, with privilege, with the pricey productions of art museums or the expensive tickets required for admission to concerts by great orchestras. We forget that some of the world's most astonishing art was produced almost thirty thousand years ago in *caves* whose walls are painted with magnificent ocher images of deer and bison. The anonymous humans who created those works did not even sign their names, for they did not yet have written alphabets, written languages. So they signed their art with handprints. Their signature became the human hand itself—and what is a hand, if not a brilliant, five-pointed star that rotates at the end of that magic wand we call an "arm"?

The cave paintings are a perfect example of beautiful art imperfectly rendered, art created by real people—hunters, cave-dwellers—who couldn't even tell us their names, who could leave only handprints as their calling card. It is *anonymous* art, art that will never be auctioned at Christie's or Sotheby's. It is *folk* art—beauty created by shaggy humans who nevertheless told us something powerful about their delight in the hunt, their reverence for the animals whose bodies gave them food, whose bones gave them tools and weapons, whose skins kept them warm. It is beauty recollected as imperfection. This, I would suggest, is the kind of beauty we need to seek in the liturgy. There is a passage in *The Book of Tea*, a classic written by the early-twentieth-century Japanese-American curator Kakuzo Okakura, that puts the matter much better than I can. Okakura wrote that *chado*, the Japanese tea ceremony, is a cult founded on the adoration of the beautiful among the sordid facts of everyday existence. It inculcates purity and harmony, the mystery of mutual charity, the romanticism of the social order. It is essentially a worship of the imperfect, as it is a tender attempt to accomplish something possible in this impossible thing we know as life.[29]

"Worship of the imperfect . . . a tender attempt to accomplish something possible in this impossible thing we know as life." In many ways, I think those words describe quite aptly what we Christians are up to when we gather for liturgy. The beauty we're looking for isn't the posed beauty of manikins in the windows of Saks or Neiman Marcus, nor is it the beauty of Mozart's *Requiem* or Haydn's *Lord Nelson Mass*. Those are great works of art, but they are not great works of liturgical art, nor are they, necessarily, testaments to the human search for justice. What we seek in Christian liturgy is the beauty that flows from the wisdom of ordinary things extraordinarily loved and valued: the hand of an eighty-year-old grandmother, a hand filled with the knowledge of all the heads it has held, cupped, comforted, cradled; the fragrance of bread and wine as they are carried in procession through the assembly and laid on the altar, food that will *become* the body and blood of Christ to *feed* the body of Christ.

We will never understand the beauty of the Christian liturgy until, as Japanese novelist Jun'ichiro Tanizaki says, we learn how to "listen to a bowl of soup." Listen to how Tanizaki describes this moment in his book *In Praise of Shadows*:

"With lacquerware there is a beauty in that moment between removing the lid and lifting the bowl to the mouth when one gazes at the still, silent liquid in the dark depths of the bowl, its color hardly differing from that of the bowl itself. What lies within the darkness one cannot distinguish, but the palm senses the gentle movements of the liquid, vapor rises from within forming droplets on the rim, and the fragrance carried upon the vapor brings a delicate anticipation. What a world of difference there is between this moment and the moment when soup is served Western style, in a pale, shallow bowl. A moment of mystery, it might almost be called, a moment of trance. . . .

"It has been said of Japanese food that it is a cuisine to be looked at rather than eaten. I would go further and say that it is to be meditated upon, a kind of silent music evoked by the combination of lacquerware and the light of a candle flickering in the dark.

[29] Kakuzo Okakura, *The Book of Tea* (Boston: Shambala, 1993) 1.

"And above all there is rice. A glistening black lacquer rice cask set off in a dark corner is both beautiful to behold and a powerful stimulus to the appetite. Then the lid is briskly lifted, and this pure white freshly boiled food, heaped in its black container, each and every grain gleaming like a pearl, sends forth billows of warm steam—here is a sight no Japanese can fail to be moved by. Our cooking depends upon shadows and is inseparable from darkness."[30]

Sometimes we have to listen to another culture in order to discover what is missing in our own. The beauty we seek in the liturgy is not necessarily the highly polished, professional excellence of a Mozart, a Haydn, a Rembrandt, a Jane Austen, but the wisdom that rises like steam from a bowl of soup, a bowl of rice. A culture's cuisine is not, after all, merely meat, fish, poultry and produce, nor is it the techniques by which these foods are seasoned and prepared. *Cuisine* is a complex act that brings food in relation to light and darkness, to architecture (a room, a space "thoughtfully prepared"), to a long cultural history of manners and mores, to tables and tableware (whether the tables are low to the floor or highly elevated), to persons living and dead. *Cuisine* is a culture's map, its mythography, its condensed symbol system.

And that is exactly what Christian liturgy is: adoration offered in spirit and truth by imperfect people making use of imperfect things, "a tender attempt to accomplish something possible in this impossible thing we know as life."

New priority # 4: **Keep perspective. Love people.** The fourth and final priority. It's time, perhaps, for us to put the liturgy in its place. When it comes to the practice of justice in our world, liturgy is neither the problem nor the solution. Recent documents such as *Liturgiam authenticam*, *Built of Living Stones*, the revised *General Instruction of the Roman Missal* 2000 are all, to one degree or another, troubling or tremendous (depending on your point of view). But none of them really deserves all the time, attention, and anxiety we give to them.

Liturgy is a humble, earthly means to an end, and the end is people—hungry people; homeless people; victims of violence, war, and oppression; children sold as slave labor; lives destroyed by disease and famine. And yes, the affluent American suburbanites as well. All these are the "end" for whom liturgy is a means. What turns our

---

[30] Jun'ichiro Tanizaki, *In Praise of Shadows* (New Haven, Conn.: Leete's Island Books, 1977) 15–17.

*Alleluia*s into dirges isn't digital pianos or Bauhaus architecture, it's our numbness, our inability to see, and hear, and touch, and embrace the end for which liturgy was created—*people*. Imperfect people, people who draw deer and bison on the walls of caves, people who sense the nearness of God in the sound of a bowl of soup, people who try to make something possible "in this impossible thing we know as life." Imperfect people are what matter; *they* are the "issue" that needs our energy and insight. Jesus did not say, "I came so that you might have authentic liturgy"; he said, "I came so you could have life—and have it abundantly, exuberantly, heaped up, and overflowing."

Dr. Nathan Mitchell is the associate director for research at the University of Notre Dame Center for Pastoral Liturgy. He is a writer for and editor of *Assembly* and *Liturgy Digest*.

6

The Transforming Power of Music:
Tales of Transformation, 200–2000

James Savage

I would like to tell some tales of transformation from the richness of our past, not so much to make us more appreciative of that vast treasury as to celebrate that glorious promise we all heard just before the *Sanctus* on the Sundays of Eastertide: "The joy of the resurrection *renews* the whole world, while the choirs of heaven sing for ever to your glory."

The "transforming power of music" is a many-splendored phrase. It can eat into the very soul of the liturgical musician or dance a bit too flippantly on the grave of the recent pseudo-psychological cliché. It can also refer to the mighty shaking up of the faithful in a specific time and place, suggesting renewal and revival.

The phrase "transforming power of music" can label for us the freshness and vitality, the clarity and immediacy, with which, over and over, throughout the history of Christian song, the music of the field, the dance floor, the village, the home, has "transformed" the music of the palace, the cathedral, the academy, the monastery. Or it can name the equal number of historic syntheses in which the sacred music of the palace, the cathedral, the academy, the monastery, has "transformed," over a period of time, the music of the village, the parish, and the home. Or it can identify the power of spirit-filled liturgical music which has transformed music in the churches by pouring the wine into new skins.

In our tales of transformation, I hope to touch on ways in which God's lavish gift of music has the power to transform the heart, the assembly, the treasury, the Church, and to keep transforming us until finally and for all eternity, "all of us," as St. Paul says, "gazing with unveiled face on the glory of the Lord, are being transformed into the same image from glory to glory, as from the Lord who is the Spirit" (2 Cor. 3:13).

NICCOLÒ
JOMMELLI

Our first tale of the transforming power of music begins in 1750. On the evening of July 28, 1750, Johann Sebastian Bach died. If you had told an internationally aware musician the next morning that Europe's greatest composer had died the night before, the response might well have been: "Oh no! Not Jommelli?" At or near the top of nearly any informed musician's list of Europe's most famous composers in 1750 would certainly have been Niccolò Jommelli (1714–1774).

Just thirty days before Bach's death, Jommelli had astounded Europe with his music for the Vatican's Vespers of Saints Peter and Paul at St. Peter's Basilica in Rome as part of the celebrations for the Great Jubilee Year 1750. The audacious thirty-five-year-old composer had created modern music featuring two hundred singers divided into eleven ensembles, each with its own continuo ensemble of organ and bassoons that were stationed around the mighty crossing of St. Peter's, with some groups even high in the cupola. A contemporary engraving depicts the mighty—"mighty" in every way—Jommelli, conducting with his roll of paper the throng of musicians on the patronal feast of St. Peter's.

Named *maestro di cappella* at St. Peter's over the strong objections of the Roman old-guard musicians, the young Jommelli, known for his modern ways of composing, was hired to provide the best possible music for the Jubilee Year. In organizing his vespers performance, Jommelli may have been responding to the challenge laid down by Pope Benedict XIV the previous year: In 1749 an encyclical had been promulgated inviting composers to provide an appropriately majestic musical framework for the liturgy. Jommelli no doubt was determined to demonstrate the possibilities under the new code to the pilgrims visiting Rome for the Holy Year. (Forty years after the encyclical's promulgation, the church in Haydn's Austria was still trying to figure it out.)

During his brief tenure as the basilica's music director, Jommelli composed nearly forty liturgical works for the papal musicians that survive in Italian libraries, a testament to their popularity. Jommelli's influence was felt not just in Italian courts and cathedrals; his contributions to the development of mid-eighteenth century art in palace and cathedral, academy and monastery, were astounding, his influence on the early classical style enormous.

These three examples will demonstrate the composer's innovations and influences:

1. The early Viennese symphonists Dittersdorf and Wagenseil credited Jommelli as the source of the emerging symphonic forms in Vienna.
2. Stamitz and the other Mannheim composers borrowed or stole directly from Jommelli the carefully notated orchestral crescendo; the clear, contrasting themes; and the four-bar phrase structure for which they are famous.
3. Everyone from Metastasio to Burney blamed or praised Jommelli for the death of the *da capo* aria.

In 1753, at the height of his international fame, Jommelli was contracted by the young ruler Carl Eugen, duke of Württemberg, to become director of music at the tiny but extravagant court in Stuttgart, a town of nearly 30,000 (at that time) in southwestern Germany. The duchy was an ecumenical anomaly. The state religion of Württemberg was Protestant, as was the State Church Council that paid the composer's salary; the duke himself, however, was a practicing Roman Catholic. As a result, the Catholic composer was obliged to provide music for both the Protestant and the Roman services—often using the same soloists, choristers, and orchestra. On more than one occasion, Jommelli conducted a *Te Deum* or

German translation of his Roman motets in a service at the major Protestant church and then packed up the entire music establishment, set up again in the palace chapel, and one hour later repeated the entire work in the context of a Catholic Mass.

And now the stage is set and we can begin our first "Tale of Transformation." This is not the sort of life-changing transformation testified to by those pilgrims to the Jubilee Year celebration at St. Peter's, nor is it the soul-shaking experience of the faithful who worshiped that day in Rome when they heard a hint of the celestial song in the glory of Jommelli's heavenly hymn. No, this is a different yet equally important aspect of the transforming power of music, the transformation that has occurred over and over in the history of the Church's song: that is, what happens when one musician, with open ear and heart—without walls or prejudice or rejection—allows the hymn of another musician from another musical style and another musical language to pierce the soul. When one musician truly listens to the song of another, allowing his or her own music to be transformed, and pours the breath of the Holy Spirit from one open vessel to another and to another. The same Spirit, different vessels.

The music of Jommelli—artistic conqueror of St. Peter's, the imperial court in Vienna, the academies of Italy and the theaters of London and Lisbon—was poured from vessel to vessel to vessel and transformed both Catholic and Protestant church music throughout southern Germany, not just in the monasteries and important churches but in villages and chapels and homes. Sitting last chair, behind all those imported Italians in the violin section of Jommelli's huge court orchestra, was Georg Eberhard Dunz (c. 1711–1775), one of the very few Germans allowed to play in the duke's orchestra. Observing his talent for popular music, Jommelli paid Dunz to compose oboe-band ditties for street dances and also programmed Dunz's cantatas at the Protestant chapel, causing Dunz to come under the spell of the Italian *Musikdirektor*.

Dunz's music remained German to the core, and his cantatas proudly showed their German Baroque roots; his music aimed for the directness of music for the dance floor, the village, and the home. Yet his music more and more reflected the master's influence. And so it was that Jommelli's modern music for Roman basilicas, Viennese opera houses, and the ducal court began to be Germanized, "folkized," *transformed* into music for the village parish.

At one of these village parishes, a very young organist named Nikolaus Ferdinand Auberlen (1755–1828) played the services, rehearsed the tiny country choir, and learned Jommelli's innovations through the church music of Dunz. With open ear and heart, without walls or prejudice or rejection, Auberlen allowed the musical prayer of another musician to pierce his soul. And so Auberlen continued the transformation: Like Dunz, he opened himself to receive and then poured the Italian composer's wine into the simpler vessels of the village church.

As Auberlen matured, he began to teach our precious art, the music of prayer as he understood it, to the children of the field and the village. One of his most eager pupils was Friedrich Silcher (1789–1860), and into *that* precocious pupil, Auberlen poured the phrasing, harmonies, structures, and melodic ideas of the now-deceased Jommelli: songs for the Church, transformed by the rhythms of the field and the piety of the home and the instruments of the local parish.

In time, the student became a teacher. When Silcher was twenty, he taught *his* understanding of music to the young in Ludwigsburg, only blocks from the house where Jommelli had once lived. At twenty-six, he was teaching in the capital, Stuttgart. At twenty-nine, he was a leading promoter of popular music in public education. At thirty-three, Silcher was known throughout the German-speaking world for his research on folk music. His folk-song arrangements were sung by newly formed community choirs throughout southern Germany. He taught that "folk song," precisely because it *was* the song of the folk, was, therefore, the most appropriate repertory to be performed by the general public, whether in the church or the school.

Today, at 212 years of age, Silcher continues to define for us what we think of as German folk music—whether we hear that music as beer-garden *om pah* or "I love to go a-wandering" or "Silent Night." It is a music that weds the innovations of Jommelli to the vitality of the German folk, the song of palace to the song of the field, the motet of the cathedral to the devotional song of the village. And it weds them so successfully that we have forgotten their debt to Jommelli.

By the early 1820s, the power of Silcher's fresh, vital folk style was being felt in Vienna. Schubert and Beethoven, and later Schumann and Mendelssohn, were touched by its honesty and vigor. And the Church is richer because of this process of transformation begun by Jommelli.

As he neared the end of his life, Franz Schubert (1797–1828) took a summer break in the composition of his monumental *Winterreise* and, responding to the urgings of his poet friend J. P. Neumann to create a Mass for the broadest cross-section of the faithful, produced his famous *Deutsche Messe* in the musical language of the people—a folk-song-styled, German vernacular setting of the Ordinary. Although the *German Mass*'s eight liturgical songs are very much in the style of Silcher, Schubert's special genius transformed the model, overflowed the vessel, and produced a prayer for the faithful that continues to touch us after nearly two centuries.

And so concludes our first tale of the transforming power of music—long in the telling but long for a reason. This same tale of transformation can be told in every time and place throughout the entire known history of Christian song: how powerful music written for palace, cathedral, academy, or monastery can transform the music of field, dance floor, home, and village parish. And how the honest vigor and clarity of the field, the dance, the village parish, and the home can teach us to sing a new language of prayer.

In fact, our second tale of the transforming power of music is a short one that takes place at the very same time, in the very same place, with the same beginning, the same ending, and the same lesson as our first tale. Just a different middle.

And that middle was Christian Friedrich Daniel Schubart (1739–1791), who studied theology at the University of Erlangen but was so frequently in trouble with the administration that he was expelled.[1] In 1763 he became the *Kantor* of the parish church in Geisslingen, a village just north of Ludwigsburg. In 1769, he was hired by Jommelli to play organ and harpsichord at the court. The exposure to Jommelli's music and music making, especially his sensitivity to text, transformed Schubart. He remembered that "no one was able to squeeze as many golden drops from the words as Jommelli."

Schubart did not pursue a career in the palace or cathedral; perhaps a ten-year imprisonment by Duke Carl Eugen for insulting one of the Duke's many mistresses played a role in this career path. During his imprisonment, Schubart developed a passion for folk lyrics and folk music. Proclaiming that "the folk song represents the true musical expression of a people," he began composing strophic and folklike Lieder, musical imitations of the songs of the field and village *but* bor-

---

[1] David Ossenkop, in *New Grove Dictionary of Music and Musicians*, 2nd ed. (hereafter *NG2*), vol. 22, 653. Throughout this essay, I have drawn on this work, one of the best scholarly reference works in any discipline. As Alex Ross wrote on July 9, 2001, in the *New Yorker*, "in the kingdom of the Grove, the great and the small, the transient and the ancient, the boring and the weird lie side by side . . . The Grove is still a magnificent achievement, and more than that, it is a work of love" (82–86).

rowing from Jommelli his sensitivity to text and his belief that "expressiveness is the golden axle around which music turns."

Beethoven, Schumann, and Schubert were fascinated by Schubart's ideas yet disagreed with him on musical issues. And so Schubert transformed Schubart's ideals, and Schubart becomes another vessel by which the golden drops of Jommelli were poured into the simplicity and expressiveness of Schubert's *Deutsche Messe*.

CHRISTIAN FRIEDRICH
DANIEL SCHUBART

So here is the moral of our first two tales: our church's music has continually renewed itself, transformed itself, because composers for nearly two millennia have listened to the "other," listened to musical languages not their own and, through this ear-opening experience, have then found new ways to sing and pray.

The philosopher Hegel could have been describing the history of our sacred song when he proclaimed his historical dialectic—thesis-antithesis-synthesis leading to thesis-antithesis-synthesis leading to thesis-antithesis-synthesis. Hegel's philosophic premise has been winningly reinterpreted as a dance in one of the great participatory rituals of the post-Vatican II era, the *Rocky Horror Picture Show*, where the processional anthem is "Let's do the Time Warp again": "It's just a jump to the left, and then a step to the right." And then—well, then straight ahead.

Again a tale of transformation from Stuttgart, not because the city has been the previously uncredited secret birthplace of musical transformation but because in moments of its history it was not unlike the towns and cities most of us come from: Milwaukee or Atlanta, Orlando or Seattle, St. Louis or San Antonio. Like most of our cities, it was not the capital city, but it certainly lay along that razor's edge where parish and preacher, musician and mystic, liturgist and layperson work out what it is to be Church.

SIXTEENTH-
CENTURY
STUTTGART

In the sixteenth century, Stuttgart was as much an ecumenical anomaly as it would be later in the eighteenth century of Jommelli. The government was Protestant; the court vacillated between Protestant and Catholic. There was a wonderful period when a principal church there was used by both Protestant and Catholic parishes. Each Sunday the priests would reconsecrate the building and altar so it could be used for Mass.

Stuttgart in the sixteenth century provides a telling tale of the transforming power of the music of the palace on the music of the home—and in turn, the music of the home on the music of the palace. It is yet another tale of the continual historic dance of the Time Warp, "just a jump to the left, and then a step to the right," but almost always moving forward.

At the beginning of the sixteenth century, Heinrich Finck, a musician with the loftiest credentials, brought glory to the court of Stuttgart with his choral four-part songs: settings of "courtly melodies" with the pre-existing tune hidden away in the tenor, surrounded by rhythmically livelier soprano, alto, and bass lines. This style of choral song—the *Tenorlied*—would provide Stuttgart musicians a model for several decades: an elegant jump to the left.

And then came Osiander. Lucas Osiander (1534–1604), like many of our current composers for the American church, was a theologian and pastor. Initially he was not an academy-trained composer but a shepherd of souls responsible for parish life and worship. Osiander of course knew the *Tenorlied* style of the court: by the mid-sixteenth century both Catholic and (the new) Protestant composers favored the tenor placement of a preexisting melody. But Osiander, enjoying the gusto of the musical middle class and the rousing community songs of the university students in Tübingen, seems to have cast his net wider than the academy and the palace. In 1569 he wrote the preface to a German-language collection of psalm settings,[2] in which he "proclaimed the importance of rendering the chorale melody understandable to the *entire* Christian communion."[3]

Fifteen years later, in 1586, Osiander published his own *Funfftzig geistlichen Lieder und Psalmen:* four-voice homophonic settings created to enable the Protestant choir and congregation to, as he said, "sing together" easily. The simple (not simplistic) harmonies were embarrassingly primitive with root position chords throughout. But the preexisting melody was moved from the previous courtly location buried in the tenor line to the easily heard, easily accompanied, easily

[2] Sigmund Hemmel's four-part *Der gantz Psalter Davids, wie derselbig in teutsche Gesand verfasset.*

[3] Walter Blankenburg, *NG2,* 18, 770.

remembered top-line soprano: one very lively step to the right. And this at the very same moment, in the very same year, that Palestrina himself published his own collection of *Hymns for the Complete Year for the Holy Roman Church*. Yet as Eberhard Stiefel reminds us in the *New Grove*, it is Osiander, not Palestrina, who is to be credited with laying the foundation for that towering edifice of Christian song, the four-part hymn with the melody and the text firmly, audibly, prominently secured in the soprano line.[4]

Osiander's foundation was so solid that Christian composers continued for centuries to build on it. The compositions of the palace, the cathedral, the academy, and the monastery were transformed. For example, Johann Hermann Schein (1586–1630), a famous composer of high art, *Kapellmeister* at the duke of Weimar's palace and later Kantor at the Thomaskirche in Leipzig, published in 1627, near the end of his life, his own tribute to Osiander's achievement. Schein's hymnal *Cantionale—Gesangbuch Augspurgischer Confession* is one of thousands of the fruits borne by the tree called Osiander. "A jump to the left, then a step to the right, a jump back to the left," but always forward.

CELTIC CHANT OF IRELAND

For our fourth tale of the transforming power of music we move back much closer to our early Christian roots—to the Celtic chant of Ireland. Belief in the power of music to change and make whole, to renew and revive, is perhaps most vibrantly attested to in surviving Irish literary tales and liturgical books—medieval sources that tell of a time when the performance of Celtic chant songs was believed to have almost sacramental power. Ann Buckley tells us that in the time before regional liturgies were completely conquered by the hegemony of the Carolingians, the singing of spiritual songs was of such cosmic importance that the very act of singing was to be considered a source of indulgence and grace. The singing of the last three strophes of a hymn was considered sufficient to earn a spiritual reward. Singing them was thought to give immunity against fire, poison, and wild animals. These songs of grace were also thought to provide protection for travelers.[5]

From our lofty twenty-first century vantage, we can shake our heads at this seeming superstition; and yet do we not fervently long for that assembly performance of the communion procession that sacramentally changes us too into the Body of Christ? Do we not pray

[4] Eberhard Stiefel, *NG2*, 24, 634.
[5] Ann Buckley, "Celtic Chant," *NG2*, 5, 343 ff.

that our song too might be a song of renewal? And is not the Communion song sung as a response to the prayer "only say the word, and I shall be healed"?

The belief in music's sacramental power led to *luas perennis,* the Celtic devotion of perpetual praise, in which part of a monastic community chanted psalms all the time. St. Patrick is said to have brought such a practice from Rome when he recommended that the *Kyrie* be sung every hour.[6] The most extreme practice of Celtic perpetual singing is recorded in the medieval Irish travelogue, the *Voyages of St. Brendan.* The sixth-century saint is reported to have encountered an island where the hymn *Ibunt sancti* was sung continuously and nonstop. The islanders were said to maintain three choirs to keep the song going.

For centuries, the Irish celebrated the power of song. Suggestions of the exuberant performance of the Celtic song repertory survive in several medieval manuscripts.

The first verse of the hymn *Cantemus in omni die* begins with a joyful description of antiphonal singing:

"Let us sing every day, chanting between two choirs,
crying out to God the worthy hymn of the holy Mary.
We should praise Mary twice,
once through the chorus here
and then through the chorus over there."

The Celtic song *Recordemur institiae* implies the use of two choirs, with a subdivided congregation providing the refrain for each of the respective choirs. Each alphabetic stanza sung by one of the choirs is followed by refrains—first one refrain for half of the assembly, then a second refrain for the other half.

Spiritus divinae lucis has a one-line refrain for the assembly following each verse.

The Exodus canticle contains repetitions of the first verse at intervals, suggesting that it was used as a response or refrain, sung by the congregation.

A vespers hymn for the Office of St. Patrick refers to alternating voices and stringed instruments:

"We chant the psalms to Christ
alternating with our strings and our voices."

---

[6] Ibid.

The Celtic church believed, no, it *knew*, that the Song of Christ was a transforming power. And so they created ways to make the song the one song of the Body of Christ with parts for the people, the trained choirs, the soloists, and the instrumentalists. Their composers created new liturgical works. Our most ancient surviving Communion song, *Sancte, venite,* is theirs.

So life-giving was the Song of Christ to these Celtic faithful that it was they who not only found new ways to sing the prayer but carefully, reverently, preserved the treasury of music that had come before them. It was those same Celtic musicians who copied our earliest surviving version of the *Te Deum.* It was they who helped preserve one of our most ancient hymns, the *Gloria.* It was their reverence for the musical expression of the past that preserved the liturgical music of their own past; e.g., the hymns of sixth-century Bangor. It is their trust in liturgical music's sacramental power that, I hope, causes us today to remember the priestly anointing we have been given as pastoral musicians.

For our fifth tale of the transforming power of music we go to Tuscany and Umbria and to the thirteenth century. Blake Wilson's article in the *New Grove* brims over with testimony to the transforming power that the medieval praise song, the *Lauda,* had on the Church and the faithful. He quotes an early instruction from Assisi that charges the singers of *Laude* to "move the hearts of the gathered to tears, more than words move the mind." Wilson even uses our word: "Devotion in Florence," he says, "was rapidly *transformed* by the dramatic rise in the number of lauda services" (emphasis mine). He traces the roots of this transforming music to St. Francis of Assisi, who admonished his followers to conclude their sermons by singing "the praises of God as minstrels of the Lord," rousing their listeners to praise God, to proclaim the divinity of the incarnate Christ, to promote the model of Mary.

This praise music was music of the street and the repertory of the lay. It was the song of revival with the rhythms of conversion. It was the language of the vernacular. No Latin here; no learned polyphony; no *Ars Antiqua* or *Ars Nova*. Both the Franciscans and the Dominicans spread their message of renewal through the power of the praise song, amplified mightily by secular bands of woodwinds and brass and drums.[7]

---

[7] One of these *laude*, transcribed and adapted by Tom Stratman, my colleague at St. James Cathedral in Seattle, has become a new "old favorite" for our outdoor Corpus Christi procession, when Christ moves among his people: a procession when we are, and are with, and are being transformed into the Body of Christ.

LUCA DELLA ROBBIA; *CANTORIA*

Of course, the composers of palace, cathedral, academy, and monastery were no fools. They too felt the power of this music, and it transformed their own music. Early in the sixteenth century, Petrucci published polyphonic *laude* composed by court composers for the palaces and cathedrals of Milan, Mantua, and Ferrara: part of the dance of the Time Warp. But, of course, history's dance requires movement in both directions in order to move ahead. And just as the composers of the palace were inspired by the vigor of the *laude*, the composers of the *laude* were inspired by the palace and began expanding their musical vocabulary toward the learned polyphonic styles.

Our last tale of music's transforming power stars a figure much better known than Osiander or Jommelli. It is the story of that extraordinary composer, poet, correspondent, natural scientist, architectural designer, preacher, and mystic: Hildegard of Bingen (1098–1179). Today we know her better than we know most of her twelfth-century contemporaries. Her *Causa et cure* is read as part of the history of medicine; her *Physica* is referred to in studies of the history of natural science; her ecstatic, idiosyncratic poetry is part of the German literature syllabus. And who can claim to know medieval music today who does not know the music of Hildegard, the Sibyl of the Rhine? Even though we have all heard her story, let's delight in sitting around the campfire and telling it one more time. If ever there was an artist who understood the possibility of transformation through the power of music, it was Hildegard.

It is reported that, sometime in her fifties, Hildegard transcribed a vision of "a celestial concert" that concluded with her famous *Ordo Virtutum* (the *Ritual of the Virtues*), a gigantic work in twelfth-century terms, with eighty-two melodies, taking over an hour to perform. Its

HILDEGARD
OF
BINGEN

very subject is transformation—transformation of the soul: transformation of a very human, very flawed soul, Anima, who, through her own sincere struggle and through the grace of God, finds union with the divine. This sung drama, with eighteen different characters vividly individualized through mode, melodic themes, range, and poetry, predates the first opera by four-and-a-half centuries.

Hildegard's musical sermon *Ordo Virtutum* begins like many of her songs, which were meditations she composed to encourage contemplation or, as she called it, *ruminatio*, rumination, the complete "chewing" of the life-altering insights she had received in visions while she was in the blinding presence of the living Light. Though *Ordo Virtutum* begins like many of her contemplative songs, the end does not come after three or four minutes. Instead "Anima," the soul, is introduced as a real here-and-now woman living the same muddled life experienced by most of us. Yet Anima is a soul truly in search of God. To strengthen her on her quest, personifications of virtues gather, one by one, in an overwhelming crescendo of increased drama until all sixteen of these virtues—manifestations of the holy life—combine to form an undefeatable protection against evil.

From page to page, Hildegard reveals her faith in the transforming power of music. The most exhilarating moment, and Hildegard's most startling musical achievement, is a sort of medieval precursor to Wagner's Brünnhilde in *Walküre*. The last actor to join her sister virtues is "Victory." Victory erupts with her medieval "Ho-Jo-To-Ho's" of joy at the very top of her range, the highest melody in the entire work, if not the entire twelfth century corpus, and—as if the celestial height of the voice were not dramatic enough—"Victory" shouts in a trumpeting Ionian: a triadic and thrilling C major after nearly an hour of more common church modes. This glossolalia of rejoicing celebrates the very moment of Anima's transformation to a state of holiness.

Perhaps the clearest indication of Hildegard's sense of the divine power of music is the treatment of her character the Devil. *He* doesn't sing a note. He only speaks. In Hildegard's cosmology a sign of complete separation from God is the unwillingness to sing, to make music.

If *New Grove* is correct, *Ordo Virtutum* was first performed by Hildegard's nuns at the dedication of their new abbey church.[8] The villagers and guests would have come that day for the expected: the divine office sung by twenty Benedictine sisters, the ancient chants, the customary psalms, the predictable hymns. But then, in Hildegard's new church, in addition to the ancient, the customary, the predictable, they were flooded with Hildegard's musical call to renewal and virtue. What must it have been like to look so deeply that day into the heavenly realm? To be able to catch for a moment the sound of the sublime? The completely other? What could those Rhinelanders have felt, if not transformation?

Hildegard's creative flow was showered on the liturgies of the Divine Office, not the Mass. Aside from one *Kyrie*, the remainder of her huge output forms a liturgical cycle to expand and intensify the prayers of matins, lauds, and vespers celebrated by the nuns. In her seventies, Hildegard undertook four preaching tours throughout the Rhineland.

[8] Marianne Pfau and Ian D. Bent, *NG2*, 11, 495.

Yet it was the nuns she left behind who actually heard Hildegard's most powerful sermons: the songs she had composed for their daily prayer.

In compiling this brief collection of tales of transformation in and through music, I chose not to return as far back as the year 200, because Edward Foley has done that in excellent fashion in his *Foundations of Christian Music*. His archeological dig among the liturgical potsherds of early Christian song should be read by every pastoral musician. In the other direction, I chose not to go beyond Schubert's 1827 *German Mass* for a very different reason. Things changed—and changed dramatically—just at the time Schubert was creating his little gem of a folk Mass. By 1830, the two sets of palace-cathedral-academy-monastery and field-dance-village-home had become no longer adequate as labels for the forces of change in the music of the Church. Of course our Time-Warp dance continued past 1830, but those sets could no longer be used as labels.

Here are a few reasons for that change in how and where music was made:

- After Schubert and Beethoven, the palace was never again to be the steady source of inspiring musical innovation.

- Monasteries grew less interested in plowing new musical ground for the Church; instead, many gradually became centers for the revival of Gregorian chant.

- Beginning about the time Schubert died concert halls began to be built for that new multiclass social phenomenon, the public. They took over positions held earlier by palace and cathedral. They became shrines in which to venerate the lofty role that concerts had come to hold in European cultural life. A Frenchman of the time reported: "One goes to the concert hall with religious devotion as the pious go to the temple of the Lord."[9]

- Many of these concert halls were built and managed as marketing tools by piano manufacturers and music publishers.[10]

- The music of the village and home underwent profound changes. For example, at the very moment Schubert was composing his *Deutsche Messe*, inexpensive and space-saving upright pianos were being developed and marketed "aimed at families living in modest homes and apartments."[11]

[9] William Weber, "Concert," *NG2*, 6, 228ff.
[10] Edwin M. Good, "Upright pianoforte," *NG2*, 26, 151.
[11] Andrew Lamb, "Music hall," *NG2*, 17, 484–85.

- 1830 saw the birth of the British music hall, which offered the working classes an evening of communal singing while they drank. In the rapidly expanding new living areas for the lower classes—the suburbs—there were also halls offering entertainment for the local working stiffs. Especially famous was the Eagle in London's City Road, immortalized in a "pop" song that many of you still know after 170 years:

"Up and down the City road,
In and out the Eagle,
That's the way the money goes . . .
Pop goes the Weasel."[12]

- As Schubert was composing his *German Mass*, "a significant development in the art of printing music, lithography, was taken up by New York publishers. It was now possible for the middle class and even the poor to own, learn, and perform the latest popular song instead of waiting to hear an itinerant musician come sing it in their village or frontier town. These inexpensive music publications reached a public quite different from the one that purchased engraved music editions." The effect as the century moved on was a "vast increase in the amount of printed music," which only began to decline as sound recordings and broadcast music of all kinds became available in the twentieth century.

For these and a host of other reasons, new pairs of influences on the Church's music have emerged, pairs that are merely suggestive and no more exact than "palace" and "field":

concert hall	"Music Hall"
university	television
this publisher	that publisher
that radio station	this radio station
this musician's organization	that musician's organization
that parish	**this parish**

In the Assisi of the Franciscans, in the Stuttgart of Osiander and Jommelli, in the Ludwigsburg of Schubart and Silcher, in the Vienna of Schubert, in the Bingen of Hildegard, when parishioners of St. Whatsername walked the mere ten or fifteen minutes to the neighboring parish of St. Whozits, they often, or even usually, heard and sang very different musical styles than those heard and sung in their home parish. The liturgy was the same Roman rite, but the musical clothing was changed—perhaps unrecognizable.

[12] "Printing and Publishing," *NG2*, 20, 370ff.

The musical differences we experience today are not new. But the tensions between practitioners of different styles seems to be. I was recently asked if I would participate in a conference to discuss the "tensions inherent in liturgical ministry; tension between a desire for a codified repertoire and a desire for a creative repertoire that reflects the diversity of time, place and culture; tension between a desire to hand on the treasury and a desire to develop a living repertoire; tension between the pursuit of excellence and an excellent pursuit of the path to holiness, in whatever form; and tension between the call to glorify God and the call to sanctify humanity."

I fear that as long as we label our differences in musical language and style—our thesis and antithesis—as "tensions"; as long as we feel that, as God's chosen elect, the music we listen to on our favorite radio station—the music of our palace or our field—is the only correct way to pray, then the dance toward synthesis in Christ's song slows to a standstill and jerks about clumsily. We must have the music of the cathedral *and* the music of the parish, if we are to continue the dance.

We are called to live out whatever the phrase "the transforming power of music" means. I hope the meaning includes the transformation that has occurred over and over in the history of the song of the Church: the transformation when one musician with open ear and heart—without walls and prejudice and rejection—allows the hymn of another musician from another musical style and another musical language to pierce the soul. When one liturgical musician listens—truly listens—to the song of another and allows his or her own music to be transformed, then such transformation becomes a pouring of the breath of the Holy Spirit from one open vessel to another and to another. Same spirit, very different vessels.

CONCLUSION

My father was an old-time Baptist preacher who could take a text—any text—and bend it to do his will, making the point he wanted to make at that moment. As an homage to him, I would like to conclude with an exegesis of today's "anthem text" in the style of my father.

We already have had the opportunity to study the first verse of today's passage: "It's just a jump to the left, and then a step to the right . . . ." So let's move to the second verse: "With your hands on your hips . . ." Here the text depicts a posture of complete vulnerability; and precisely because it is so confidently vulnerable, it is the posture of assurance, the stance of belief, the attitude of boldness.

The verse continues: "You bring your knees in tight . . . ." Here the author is saying: "Prepare yourself!" or, as the Pauline author tells us in Ephesians: "Stand therefore, having your loins girt about with truth." Or again, as St. Peter writes: "Wherefore gird up the loins of your mind, be sober, and hope to the end."

The next verse is more difficult: "But it's the pelvic thrust . . . ." That is, from the very center of your being, with your whole body, your whole mind, your whole soul, with your entire emotional self, move forward, and never, as did Lot's wife, look back.

Then comes: "that starts to drive you insane . . ." From the context we know "insane" is not meant to be negative. Here it is used to mean "bliss." And we are only at the beginning of the race toward bliss. The text says, "that starts to drive." The beginning of the race is sometimes difficult and bumpy, and we get off to a slow start, but victory comes to those who keep their eyes fixed firmly on the goal.

And then those familiar words of the last verse: "let's do the Time Warp again." That is, once you have done all of this, my brothers and sisters, it is time to do it over. This is a never-ending call to continual renewal. To do it again. And the text repeats: "let's do the Time Warp again." Notice the first-person plural imperative. "Let us." It is no longer "you." It is a summons to "do" together, not divided into you and me, but together: a "we" that embraces the differences of cathedral practice and parish practice, inner city and suburban, African-American and Korean-American Catholics, that includes both a jump to the left and a step to the right in a single dance.

Let *us* do the Time Warp again.

Dr. James Savage is the director of music ministries at St. James Cathedral, Seattle. He has been a distinguished visiting artist at the University of Washington and a Fulbright Fellow in liturgical music.

7

All at Once the Music Changed: Reflections on Liturgical Music in the United States Since Vatican II

John Foley, S.J.

I am glad to attempt the task of this Hovda Lecture: an overview of liturgical music in the United States since Vatican II. Of course, many difficulties attend such a task. In historical terms we are still very close to Vatican II and its changes, and coherent history is difficult to write through a magnifying glass. Moreover, I myself have been part of all the phases of liturgical music development, and so must work to avoid unwarranted bias.

This latter difficulty may prove an advantage. As a participant I have experienced the topic in a way that can also bring about a more informed viewpoint, limited though it still might be. Thus I might well be able to give a guided tour of recent liturgical musical history in its most readily viewable areas, trying to find the impulses and composers that have had particular influence. As an addition to this "fly-over" methodology, I would like to add as best I can a non-exclusive evaluation of each period of development, and sometimes of certain examples from that period.

I have mentioned periods of development. These must be arbitrarily assigned. They can bring clarity if not taken too seriously. In formulating them, I rely on research, my own memory and estimation, and also on an as-yet unpublished paper given by Jan Michael Joncas at the 1998 Liturgical Composers Forum in St. Louis.[1]

I designate the first period as 1965 to nearly 1980, noting that the force of that period still exists. It was the time in the Church when the

---

[1] Joncas, *"Where We Have Been: Roman Catholic Liturgical Music in the United States Since Vatican II,"* delivered at the national Liturgical Composers Forum, sponsored by the Center for Liturgy at Saint Louis University, January 26–29, 1989. Joncas presents numerous features of these years including consideration of Church documents, not just or mainly a history of music.

changes were the most shocking and the liturgical assembly and its leadership were most receptive to the new popular music. The second period, from around 1975 to 1990 could be called the period of "increased sophistication"—a term coined by Joncas. In the third period, 1990 to the present, musicians have been paying more attention to liturgy's ritual dimension, to the classical tradition, and to music for youths.

PERIOD 1: 1965–1975, SOME SHOCKING CHANGE, SOME CONTINUATION AS BEFORE

The Second Vatican Council set up a tension that is still in the process of working itself out. For one thing, it called us to preserve the "sacred treasury of music."[2] But, secondly the council also called for a wider use of the vernacular,[3] and thirdly it told us that "full and active participation by all the people is the aim to be considered before all else."[4] How to bring all three of these together in a music that would be available for use not in ten years but now?

One interpretation underlay most "new liturgy": the entire assembly is the worshiping body. Though the priest of course exercised an irreplaceable role, Mass "belongs" to all members, each according to his or her role. People in the pews were to participate fully, consciously and actively. All are genuinely part of the assembly.

Many questions followed. Many psyches, life styles, cultural differences, etc., entered into the interpretation of Council demands. "Full participation" by the people obviously suggested music with words in the vernacular. But this was mostly missing from the sacred treasury of music of the Roman Catholic Church's received (European) tradition. Moreover, some asked how music could be "of the people" and simultaneously lie mainly in the classical tradition of sacred music? Symphonic music by no means attracts the majority of Americans. Or is liturgy mainly a restricted zone where what is formally "Church" music reigns, as opposed to musical styles ported in from popular culture?

Such questions were debated, but the real answer was already being given in the music and texts composers were writing. How can music come together with the people? Let us look.

---

[2] Constitution on the Sacred Liturgy, #114.
[3] Op. Cit., #36.
[4] Op. Cit., #14, 28, 30.

Classical Response

Composers such as Jan Peter Vermulst (1925–1994) were writing classically, but they were writing for the people, for communal participation. By the way, I am using the word "classical" throughout this talk to refer to choral and organ music of the more "high style," that is, church music comparable to the varieties of classical concert music. Vermulst was already a famous concert composer in his native Netherlands, and he wrote prodigiously. After Vatican II he also began to write "accessible" music for the new order of Mass. His "Holy," from the *Mass of Christian Unity* is still quite familiar to Catholics in this country. It was copyrighted in 1964 but is still part of the 2001 edition of *We Celebrate*, heir to the well-known *Peoples Mass Book*, published by World Library, as is his setting of the "People's Mass," composed in 1970, and the magnificent Alleluia called "Praise God in This Holy Dwelling" (1964). *Peoples Mass Book* was published early enough (1955) and with enough vision that its positioned World Library as the first main supplier of music in English after Vatican II.[5]

Vermulst's Holy is almost completely in the pentatonic scale, which of course reflects a traditional folk approach to music, and which sounds familiar just because it is in that scale. Simply put, the pentatonic scale consists of the five black keys in an octave span on the piano. However, for contrast, Vermulst used some alternating phrases that contained some of the "white keys" on the piano. This created a smooth, scale-like contrast to the more strictly pentatonic phrases. It is a fine melodic strategy, worthy of a composer of Vermulst's stature. Simple tunes are the most difficult to write, so the saying goes.

There were other successful approaches to a people's music that tended toward the classical. Joseph Gelineau's "My Shepherd Is the Lord," for instance, is one of the most aesthetically pleasing, perfectly constructed pieces of music. It was probably composed in the 1950s during his doctoral studies. For it and other psalms, he derived a new way of singing the syllables. Instead of writing a new melody for each verse (since syllables of one "verse" did not match those of the next) or *recto tono*, such as that used in the traditional Gregorian chant, he devised a melody of whole note durations, each note of which would handle one stressed syllable, along with up to three more unstressed ones. The result was a more graceful and beautiful way of chanting

---

[5] *Peoples Mass Book* contained among many other hymns:, "Keep in Mind" by Lucien Deiss, "To Jesus Christ, Our Sovereign King," with words by the famous St. Louis liturgist Msgr. Martin Hellriegel, and the whole of Vermulst's *Mass for Christian Unity*.

words, while providing a way to be uniquely true to actual psalm. Gelineau did his settings first for the Hebrew, then in French, then used his settings with an English translation from The Grail.[6]

One problem with using the Gelineau tones in this country is that most American cantors think metrically. Therefore they try to sing this kind of music as if it were in, say, 4/4, and that is not what Gelineau had in mind. Another is that the newer publications of his music feature refrains freshly written by a new group of composers. Not all the original refrains were great or easy, but quite a few were. It is a shame to lose, for instance, the remarkable Refrain of the "My Shepherd Is the Lord" refrain, written by Gelineau.

At this same time in Holland, a revolution was in progress. The Dutch Catechism had just been published. Was it doctrinally correct in all ways? Rome didn't think so. The music that emerged from this ferment in Holland was composed by people such as Bernard Huijbers and Huub Oosterhuis. Their collaborations sparked the composers of the "Dutch School," who believe that music must be simple, that the assembly must be viewed as a "Performing Audience" (the title of Huijber's best known book) and that the music must bring to life what it celebrates.

And there isn't a Catholic in the world who doesn't know the Belgian Lucien Deiss's "Keep in Mind." As congregations sing it, they automatically go into harmony in the second half. This is just one of hundreds of pieces written by Father Deiss. At Vatican II Deiss was an adviser to the Committee writing the Constitution on the Sacred Liturgy, and his music is an outgrowth of his research and wisdom.

Folk-Popular

A second response from liturgical musicians in the United States was to bring forth not only vernacular texts but also vernacular music, by which I mean compositions with indigenous popular appeal and sentiment. At first this strategy was relatively unrefined and small in scope. It featured the guitar, which high school and college students could play almost without training. Folk-style music gave a freedom from complication to those who wished to write their own music. On the radio, sounds of the Kingston Trio, the Brothers Four, the New

---

[6] Coincidentally, this method bears resemblance to the theory of the poet Gerard Manley Hopkins, who changed the course of modern poetry by his theory of "sprung rhythm." There, too, like children's nursery rhymes (or Gelineau psalms), there could be various numbers of unstressed syllables between the fixed number of stresses in a line of poetry.

Christie Minstrels and others of the so-called folk music movement were still enjoying popular success in the early to middle 60s; "hootenannies" were frequent. Pop-folk sounds began to waft through Pope John XXIII's newly opened window.

This kind of music was represented in the Hymnal for Young Christians prepared by F.E.L. Publications. This company started life as "Friends of the English Liturgy," under the aegis of Dennis Fitzpatrick. The contents of the hymnal were divided into entrance songs, offertory songs, Communion songs, general liturgical songs, and a surprising final category—catechetical songs. Since the book was designed to be an ecumenical "supplement to adult hymnals," it had also a "Roman Catholic music supplement" that included Mass settings, including the *Missa Bossa Nova*. Simple enthusiasm played a key role.

Influence of the Four-Hymn Mass

Much music of this time fits into the pre-conciliar phenomenon of the "four hymn Mass," a use of vernacular hymnody that goes back to the early twentieth century. Before Vatican II, the high Mass, usually celebrated on only Sundays and major feasts, was sung chorally in Latin. Singing in the vernacular was not allowed. The high Mass was large in scope and was marked by multiple ministers, many candles and much ceremony. In contrast, low Mass had no music of its own and was, in fact, a scaled down version of the high Mass, a practical measure to allow more frequent celebrations. In response to the request of liturgists, permission was given to sing vernacular hymnody at low Mass, but only at the "soft spots," that is, portions of the Mass where nothing else by way of official text or action was taking place: before the priest began the liturgy, at the time of the offertory; during Communion (since few people received Communion, anyway), and when the priest had finished Mass.

The result has sometimes been described in jest as the "hymn sandwich." When folk/popular music began its new life in the parishes, of course it followed this layered approach. Several decades later the name "occasional music" would become attached to it, because instead of setting the established liturgical moments for musical/ritual prayer—which its four-hymn Mass origins had forbidden it to do—it produced prayerful music that fit in between the more ritually invested moments.

A look at some of the popular music of these early years will illustrate. "Hear, O Lord, the Sound of My Call"—one of Ray Repp's lasting pieces; Willard Jabusch's "Whatsoever You Do to the Least of my

Brothers"; Bob Fabing's "Be Like the Sun"; Clarence Rivers's "God Is Love." Though the latter was at times sung as a memorial acclamation, still the character of these songs was occasional, non-ritual and meant to fit into, for example, the Preparation of the Gifts, Communion or Post-Communion, Opening or Closing: in other words, into the four-hymn Mass's occasional music locations.

New indigenous music for vernacular texts had also another characteristic worth mentioning. Like the music on popular radio stations of the day, the music tended to be ephemeral. No matter how good or beloved a "top ten" piece is, sooner or later (usually sooner) it drops off the charts to be replaced by some other new composition. Thus the market for popular music could be maintained indefinitely, since it had a self-replacing inventory. The same would prove true for popular liturgical music.

Some of this early music is still in use, however. Sebastian Temple's "Make Me a Channel of Your Peace" became a favorite of Princess Diana and was played at her funeral in London long after its original popularity. The melodic strategy of this piece is simple and to some objectionable: recitative. Most of the melody is based on the repetition and frequent return to the same note or a nearby neighbor of that note. Happily, the contrasting "bridge," as it is called in the music trade, at last escapes the narrow selection of notes. This is good strategy, and perhaps it can be said that the piece has lasted because it is so simple and because its composition technique is not bad. Does this piece serve the ritual? Probably not, though it would be fine in a four-hymn Mass setting.

The Composing/singing group called the Dameans had their remote beginnings in 1968 as Darryl Ducote, Mike Balhoff, Dave Baker, Buddy Ceaser, and Gary Ault began to write music in the popular contemporary folk idiom for use in the New Orleans area. They gradually expanded their repertory and by 1973 were writing such lasting songs as "We Praise You, O Lord," and "Bread, Blessed and Broken."

Liturgico-musical values

One pungent criticism of the folk/poplar music of this period came from the professional composer, Ed Summerlin. Speaking at the 1967 North American Liturgical Week,[7] Summerlin regretted the emergence of music of poor taste and quality.

---

[7] The Liturgical Weeks are beginning to recede from popular consciousness, but they played a most important role in the development of liturgical reform. The first week opened

"If we want folk music let's use the real folk music of our lives . . . . Let's use Simon and Garfunkel's 'I am a Rock,' 'The Dangling Conversation,' and the Beatles' 'Nowhere Man,' 'Help,' and 'A Day in the Life.' At least this is contemporary folk music that has some integrity and authenticity. It is not as pleasant as we might like—but then, neither is being a Christian."[8]

Summerlin, then experimenting with jazz as a mode for liturgical music, found the nascent folk/popular movement lacking in musical and lyrical value. His devaluation is interesting because the alternatives which he, perhaps mockingly, suggested would take liturgical music still farther from the ritual and indeed from Christianity in general.

One of the lasting values throughout the entire history of music in the Church has been creativity. The creativity and ability of all persons have been with the Church since its beginning. People endowed with special gifts are eager to give what they have to the communal worship enterprise. Despite the real drawbacks in the early folk influenced music, it allowed creativity. The popular model of creativity that appeared in church music in 1965–1966 was one that sent this message: "You, too, can write a tune. Got a guitar? You can write a tune." The music as well as the text, in this pop music model, had to be something that would "reach" everyone. It also allowed communal, personal prayer. Communal because it helped us, through song, to emphasize that we're here together, we all get to pray together. It's not "the performer's music," it's ours.

At the time that Vermulst composed his *Mass of Christian Unity*, F.E.L. had just begun, and North American Liturgy Resources (NALR) had not yet been organized. World Library of Sacred Music began in the early 1950s. Omer Westendorf began compiling, revising, and writing texts for an English-language hymnal, so that, by 1964, when the Mass was first celebrated in English as a result of Vatican II reforms, he was the only Catholic music publisher ready with a hymnal

in Chicago on October 21, 1940, and yearly conferences continued until 1975. What began as a small gathering of hundreds in the basement of the Cathedral church of Chicago became by 1964 a vast assembly of 20,000 people in St. Louis's Keil Auditorium! The lists of speakers for these weeks would read like a who's who of the North American liturgical movement. The weeks began under the auspices of the "Benedictine Liturgical Conference," which by 1943 became simply "The Liturgical Conference," and which still exists today.

[8] From *Experiments in Community*, proceedings of the Twenty-eighth North American Liturgical Week, held in Kansas City, Missouri (Washington, D.C.: The Liturgical Conference, 1967) 37.

as mentioned above. His company distributed more than two million copies of the *Peoples Mass Book* in three years.

PERIOD 2: 1975–1990, INCREASED SOPHISTICATION, SCRIPTURE FOR CATHOLICS

The second period, from 1975 to about 1990 (I chose the latter date arbitrarily), can be called a period of "increased sophistication," and also represents the entrance of scripture into the normal song of the Catholic Church. During this period we moved away from the four-hymn Mass. The first edition of *Music in Catholic Worship* by the Bishops' Committee on the Liturgy appeared in 1972 and began to be noticed in the parishes as a few years went by. Its classification of the musical elements in the Mass[10] began to tease parishes away from the four-hymn Mass on the one hand and the centuries-old Mass settings for choir, organ and/or orchestra on the other. The latter had little if any space for participation by parts of the assembly other than the musicians; the former little regard for liturgical structure.

Jesuit Music

The Folk/Popular field began to burgeon. Instead of scattered publications, diligent attempts at creating liturgical music began to take shape. The present author had written in 1964 a piece entitled "For You Are My God," which was not to find publication for some years, but which traveled through Catholic circles by means of the rather primitive duplication methods of that period. After a number of years the young composer was surprised to find that the Catholic Charismatic Movement had taken this piece as their anthem, and even sang it at the huge conference at Notre Dame Stadium. Though he was a classically trained composer, the author saw a need for more "music of the people," one logical outcome of Vatican II, and wrote a large number of such pieces.

By 1971 other Jesuits had done the same, but had not been in communication with one another. Sheer coincidence brought a number of these together for studies at Saint Louis University. A private publication of nearly sixty pieces ensued, copied out by hand by Dan Schutte. The publisher North American Liturgy Resources (NALR), which had just formed in Cincinnati in 1970, heard about the "St. Louis music"

[9] Jan Michael Joncas, *op. cit.*

[10] Acclamations, processional songs, responsorial psalms, ordinary chants, and supplementary songs.

and asked to publish it. *Neither Silver nor Gold* came out in 1973. The sub-title of this collection described it simply as *"Liturgical Music by St. Louis Jesuits.* Inadvertently this subtitle had supplied a name for the new composers' group, from then on known as "The St. Louis Jesuits." Eventually called "The Jesuits," the men each wrote their own music, but gave critique to one another, and released recordings that included music from each. NALR was happy to encourage the Jesuit music, since they already published Carey Landry, whose music (the *Hi, God!* series of children's music, "Set Me Like a Seal," "Hail Mary, Gentle Woman") was already very popular. Landry has continued to compose and record with great success up to this day, though he notes that his music is not primarily liturgical in nature. In a few years NALR became prosperous enough to relocate in Phoenix, Arizona, in a large, newly built plant.

Though their music often was fitted into the four-hymn format, nevertheless, the Jesuits also gave attention to ritual moments of the liturgy. Bob Dufford and Dan Schutte wrote the widely used "Holy" of what is now called the *St. Louis Jesuits Mass.* Dufford also wrote an as yet unpublished Preface that is still widely known by many presiders.

Four values formed the music of these Jesuits—Dufford ("Be Not Afraid"), John Foley ("One Bread, One Body"), Tim Manion ("Gentle Night"), Roc O'Connor ("Lift Up Your Hearts"), and Schutte ("Here I Am, Lord"). First, the use of Scripture as inspiration for the words. This was inspired at first by the present author's love of Joseph Gelineau's psalm settings, but was not intended as a repetition of prose translations of the Bible. Some pieces such as "For You Are My God" were versifications of Scripture (following the Protestant and Anglican tradition of versified psalms) which attempted close fidelity to the original. Others were "based on" a Scripture text, concentrating on the meaning but allowing a distance from close translations. Finally, there were "meditations" upon a passage.

Second, the combination of spirituality and popular melodic content in liturgical music. Young in Ignatian spirituality, still the Jesuits felt the connection of scriptural contemplation and music for the Mass. Dan Schutte began the practice of longer, highly melodic refrains, which became a characteristic of much of the group's music. Third, from the beginning the Jesuits added to the popular music format by use of choral singing in Refrains and at times in verses as well. They combined this traditional church sound with elements of popular music.

Sometimes they used organ, but most often instruments such as guitar, piano, bass, flute, oboe and strings. O'Connor in particular introduced "up-tempo" music featuring the drum-set. Four, recordings of the music, which had begun mainly and merely as teaching devices, began to become popular on their own. Because of the spiritual and scriptural content, Catholics at large found them helpful for their own development as Christians, both within liturgy and outside it. The music became highly popular especially for about ten years. The Jesuit music coalition stopped working together in about 1985, but four out of the five composers continue writing and publishing today.

The Road Beyond

The popularity of Jesuit music opened a way for the popular liturgical music movement, sometimes referred to as "contemporary." Such music, not intended as a rebuke to classical/organ/choir music, nevertheless did seem to do exactly that. It used traces of the whole range of popular music styles, on the understanding that cultural music of such prominence would give congregations music already their own, music that already existed alongside classical orchestral music as well as classical Church music. As a result, NALR expanded and began the popular hymnal called *Glory and Praise*. F.E.L. sued the Archdiocese of Chicago for illegal copying of its music in parishes, and they won.[11]

In 1979 Michael Joncas published "On Eagle's Wings." This piece is another of the "perennials" to come out of the period. It usually tops the list of most popular liturgical songs in the United States, along with "Be Not Afraid," "Here I Am," and "One Bread, One Body." The compositional tools used by the composer are interesting, especially since they occur in a so-called "folk" genre piece. The melody of "On Eagle's Wings" begins with what theorists call an unprepared dissonance (on the downbeat): that is, with a note that is not in the chord that accompanies it, but "resolves" downward into that chord in the succeeding

---

[11] "In 1972, F.E.L. Publications entered into a legal battle to make the issue visible. It sued the Archbishop of Chicago for massive copyright infringement within the parishes of the diocese. This was the beginning of an encounter that has become part of Catholic myth and folklore. People remember confiscating books, destroying song-sheets, and being forbidden to even sing F.E.L. songs from memory. They also remember the size of the settlement: $3 million dollars." From "An Ethical Spotlight on Unauthorized Copying of Liturgical Music within the Catholic Church," by M. Hettinger. Available on the internet at http://members.iglou.com/hettingr/maggie/ClassPapers/UnauthorizedCopy.html

note. Critics surely would have said that such a beginning would be impossible for congregations, but not so. When the refrain arrives, Joncas uses the same melodic strategy he began with, only in inversion. That is, the first downbeat of the refrain, on the word "bear," of "bear you up," is again an unprepared dissonance, but is this time resolved upward. The selection of chords is interesting. The tune starts on the sub-dominant, which resolves to the tonic, an unusual move for a melody of the popular variety. What is more, the tonic chord, usually the most unadorned of all, is a major seventh chord. Such sophistication is far from the criticism that popular church songs rely on I-IV-V harmonies only (or in other words, that they use only the three most simple chords). Joncas has continued to write and publish music and has as well made significant contributions to liturgical scholarship.

GIA, which began as the "Gregorian Institute of America" in 1941 and became simply "GIA Publications, Inc." in 1968, had by this time accumulated a large catalog of classical and chant publications, mainly in sheet music or "octavo" form. In 1971 the first edition of *Worship: A Complete hymnal and Mass Book for Parishes* came out and has been through many iterations since then. In the early 1980s GIA elected to enter the popular music field. NALR's widespread success with *Glory and Praise* had shown the felt need in Catholic Churches for a folk/popular hymnal. GIA determined to build a new hymnal, *Gather*, as an approach to this same market. They began seeking out composer-artists to supply the repertory. The St. Louis Jesuits were nearing the end of their long-lasting work together and for that reason declined the invitation. But the successors to the Jesuits' popularity were waiting in the wing. Michael Joncas, who moved from NALR to GIA, Marty Haugen, and David Haas.

Haugen and Haas first came to popularity first with the publication in 1983 of *Psalms for the Church Year*. The quality of these pieces was generally high and a significant number of them remain in the repertory today. The seeds of a new period of church music were contained in this publication. Far from being occasional songs for the four-hymn Mass, or what had come to be called "service music" by publishers (Holy, Memorial Acclamation, Amen), *Psalms* represented a concerted focus on ritual moments of the Mass and Prayer of the Hours. The pieces were easy for congregations, but possessed a melodic appeal—as well as brevity—that made them the new successes of American liturgy. Haugen published a second edition of *Psalms* five years later. When the hymnal *Gather* came out it used these settings as psalmody for the Responsories.

Joncas, Haas and Haugen began performing their music together around the country, but wrote and recorded on their own for the most part. One of the most salient examples is Haugen's *Mass of Creation*, written in 1984. Haugen took care to write for both the guitar ensemble and for keyboard, publishing eventually a separate and different organ arrangement. The simplicity of the melody for the Holy is a matter of construction, seen best by a more detailed analysis than is possible here. In short, it represents a pattern of rising and falling notes within a five-note interval. This economy of means is one reason for the world-wide popularity of the setting. Another is its manageable length and its readily graspable rhythms.[12]

The mixture of commercial earnings and music for the Church is a necessary element of the popular type of liturgical music that had fully emerged by this time. This mixture has been viewed with suspicion by classical and ritual liturgists, and also by those in favor of traditional choral works. Mark Searle questioned the reason for the proliferation of music that has resulted. This is possibly answered by the rational of popular music: to be popular for a while and then be replaced by other music. In any case, the values of such music, at least from this period, seem to this author to outweigh the criticism.[13]

In 1978 the first recording and printed music from an ecumenical community outside of Taizé, France, came out in the United States. The concept for this unique form of congregational song was developed by the late Brother Robert, one of the early members of the community. He gathered and prepared the texts, sent them to Jacques Berthier, organist and composer at St-Ignace, the Jesuit church in Paris, with rather specific guidelines which Berthier met admirably. Not only did this music include words from many languages, but its contemplative nature was based on the ancient principle of mantra repetition. In this style, a melody of up to several lines is sung repeatedly without interruption by an entire assembly, creating a certain meditative or even mesmerizing effect. At times verses or instrumental melodies are sung or played at the same time. *Veni Sancte Spiritus* is an especially effective example.[14]

---

[12] Beethoven's famous melody for the "Ode to Joy" in the Ninth Symphony, fourth movement, lies entirely within the interval of a fifth, with the exception of one note, which note provides simple but profound variety.

[13] For more reflections on this question, cf. my "Why Are They Writing All This Music?", in *Postmodern Worship & the Arts* (2002: Resource Publications, San Jose, Calif.) 117–27.

[14] The Taizé community itself consists of around a hundred brothers from different Christian traditions, but who live together following a monastic tradition of prayer,

An important new force in popular church music came to the fore in this era. Oregon Catholic Press (OCP), which began 1870 as publisher of the Portland, Oregon, *Catholic Sentinal* newspaper and became the Catholic Truth Society of Oregon in 1922, in 1980 acquired its present name and began its publication of liturgical music.

Classical Church Music

In the period 1980–1994, Richard Proulx was organist/music director at the historic Cathedral of the Holy Name in Chicago, after spending ten years (1970–1980) at Saint Thomas Church, Medina/Seattle. He is a widely published composer of more than three hundred works, including congregational music in every form, sacred and secular choral works, song cycles, two operas, and instrumental and organ music. He remains an important and prolific composer for the Church.

Alexander Peloquin (1919–1997) spent more than forty years as organist/choir director at the Cathedral of St. Peter and St. Paul in Providence, Rhode Island, and thirty-nine years as composer in residence and choral director at Boston College. "He was the first person to really take up the task of writing [liturgical] music in English and for the modern Church," Richard Proulx has said. Peloquin made a point of composing melodies containing simple refrains for the congregation to sing, and utilized elements from jazz to Broadway. Pieces such as "Gloria of the Bells," still a top-selling item in the GIA catalog, and his "Lyric Mass," together with 319 choral octavos in print, make Peloquin one of the most influential composers not only in this period but beyond.

In 1970, composer Robert Blanchard (1932–2002) established the Composers' Forum for Catholic Worship, Inc. For seven years this organization acted as a center for liturgical research and a publisher of music for Post-Vatican II music. The Forum emphasized the development of artistic, liturgically valid music for congregation, cantor and choir. Blanchard himself wrote not only liturgical music but also symphonic.

World Library, by this time purchased by J. S. Paluch Company and re-named World Library Publications, Inc. (WLP), continued its strategy of quality music for the people, which included Masses, octavos, the music of Lucien Deiss, and perhaps culminating with the well-known hymn by Westendorf and Robert Kreutz, "Gifts of Finest Wheat."

---

work, and hospitality. Its week-long retreats attract thousands of people, especially between the ages of 17 and 30. What became known as "Music from Taizé" became over the next decade a standard for certain moments in Catholic liturgies.

By the last decade of the twentieth century, Catholic Church music had moved well along from its first period after Vatican II. For one thing, the sheer amount of music being published began to challenge the local musician and liturgist with the impossible task of even sampling the new pieces, much less of putting them to use. For another, the trend toward creating music that fits into the ritual showed that only so many Mass settings or psalm settings can be accommodated. Moreover, cultural diversity began to show itself as quite important, so that different styles were needed for different groups. The importance of the classical and neo-classical tradition of Catholic Church music has itself come to the fore, with emphasis on training and competence in both liturgy and music. This includes an emphasis on organ as the primary instrument of accompaniment for liturgical song. Finally, there is no longer a dearth of music for the new liturgy, just the opposite. The time of liturgical music "heroes" was beginning to pass.

In the early 1990s Oregon Catholic Press bought NALR. The latter pioneer publisher had begun to experience the uncertainties of the marketplace in Phoenix and decided to become a subsidiary of OCP. This move brought music of the St. Louis Jesuits, Michael Joncas, and Carey Landry into the OCP fold. World Library experienced a rejuvenation under its parent organization, J. S. Paluch Company, longtime publisher of *We Celebrate* missalette. GIA, OCP, and WLP remain the three major publishers of Catholic liturgical music today.

A good number of composers, even some who had been active in Period One, have moved along with the times and are still writing. Richard Proulx has continued to arrange, conduct and compose music for the church. Lucien Deiss has maintained his scholarship and his music writing, represented here in the United States by the influential liturgical dancer, Gloria Weyman. Steven C. Warner, who began the Notre Dame Folk Choir in 1980 began publication of recordings and music by the greatly expanded Choir in 1995 at WLP. Dan Schutte has continued to compose occasional pieces for Mass (e.g., "Holy Darkness") as well as Mass and Easter Vigil settings. Bob Hurd, who began publishing in the days of F.E.L. in the First Period, has continued to publish in a variety of styles, which diversity he believes is crucial to liturgy. Bob Dufford and Roc O'Connor are still writing and publishing, as is the present author. I have two collections with GIA and four with OCP. There has been no ceasing of the publication and popularity of Marty Haugen's music, nor of David Haas's. Utilization of their music seems to increase as the years go by, rather than decrease. Grayson Warren Brown continues to publish, perhaps reaching his greatest success in a long career during this latest period. And the music of the St. Louis Jesuits continues to be used and to sell quite briskly.

Moving Closer to the Ritual

Through the categories provided by *Music in Catholic Worship* years before, liturgical leaders and composers began to classify liturgical music by its function as well as by its style. Acclamations, processional songs, responsorial songs, ordinary chant, supplementary songs, and more, provided, especially in this period, true alternatives to the four-hymn Mass. New settings of the Mass had been coming out since the *Peoples Mass Book*, which in 1966 featured settings by Jan Vermulst, Howard Hughes, Robert Kreutz, and Henry Papale, among others. But now the *Mass of Creation*, having reigned for almost ten years, began to be suspected of approaching senility. Oregon Catholic Press in 1996 therefore published eight new Masses at once, including the *Celtic Mass* by Christopher Walker, *Mass of the Pilgrim Church* by the present author, Mass parts by Dan Schutte in the collection *Always and Everywhere*, and a Jamaican Mass by Richard Ho Lung. By the end of the 1990s *Psalms for the Church Year* had reached volume ten and Mass of Creation remains the most used Mass in the world.

And at this point publishers also were beginning to bring out music for liturgical units instead of for simply discrete parts of Mass. In 1988 David Haas had already released a two-volume collection, *Who Calls You by Name: Music for Christian Initiation*, while OCP's Christopher Walker brought out *Christ, We Proclaim*, for musicians, liturgists and catechists in RCIA. There is now music especially written for funerals and healing, for Morning and Evening Prayer (which of course had been approached for decades by composers). Marty Haugen and Gary Daigle have brought out *The Church Gathers: for the Gathering Rite*. It attempts to provide complete musical settings for the opening rite from the Sign of the Cross to the opening prayer, using contemporary music that has already found prominence. Bob Hurd's Mass setting *Ubi Caritas* provides a nearly through-sung settings of the gathering rite. Time will tell whether this approach will find popularity and lead to envisioning the opening rite itself as one united musical ritual.

Chant, which for at least twelve centuries had provided music solely oriented toward setting the words of the liturgy, now is experiencing a revival. This renewal cannot be called major to the same extent that popular contemporary music can, yet its very presence is significant. GIA features recordings, especially under Richard Proulx' direction, and publications of chant music. OCP has published *Lord, Open My Lips,* by Cyprian Consiglio, for liturgy of the hours, based on the Camaldolese chants arranged by and in many cases written by Fr. Cyprian. These melodies are approachable by non-musical worshippers, but contain good melodies and an ingenious approach to recitative tones. Bob Hurd has produced a chant recording, *Ubi Caritas,* a Mass setting based on the famous chant melody, and including his own new chant setting of *Ubi Caritas.*

Howard Hughes has published nearly seven hundred works since 1968 and has written a great deal of unpublished music for use within his own community. His interest has always been in liturgical settings for organ and congregation/cantor, and he has been very successful over all the years. His psalm tones were used for the Liturgical Training Publications (LTP) publication of the International Commission on English in the Liturgy (ICEL) psalm translations.[15]

There have also been collections concentrating on specific seasons. Lent, Triduum and Easter are covered by Ricky Manalo's *Beyond the Days,* which combines simplicity of melody together with a truly liturgical approach. *Behold the Glory of God, Music for the Easter Vigil* by Roc O'Connor, features a bold re-mythologizing of the liturgy, with African rhythms. Many other examples could be given.

Classical Tradition and Youth Music Innovation

Neo-classical music for the liturgy continues to be written, with some new names entering the forum. James Chepponis, a priest of the Pittsburgh Diocese and Music Director at Pittsburgh's St. Paul Cathedral, has over sixty publications with GIA for organ and choral resources. Charles Callahan of St. Paul, Minnesota, Leo Nester and Lynn Trapp have music with various publishers. British composer, Paul Inwood, a graduate of the Royal School of Music, writes in a popular version of classical tradition. Christopher Willcock, an Australian and student of Joseph Gelineau at the University of Paris, at last brought a

---

[15] *Psalms For Morning And Evening Prayer* (Chicago: Liturgy Training Publications, 1995). These translations were subsequently withdrawn by the United States Conference of Catholic Bishops, and publication ceased.

number of his over four hundred published titles of liturgical and concert music to the United States. These include music for Masses, funerals, funeral services, and so on, published by OCP. One of the very interesting newer composers is Bob Moore. He writes music in various paradigms but mainly his classically-based instrumental and sung music is an important addition to the repertory. John Schiavone has emerged as a successor to the famous Italian Masses prior to Vatican II. Schiavone's writing is of course crafted for the renewed liturgy and for assembly participation, but it is well written and in the classical tradition.

Almost at a polar opposite is the youth music movement. If, in a former era, the St. Louis Jesuits had seemed an opposite to traditional music, now music for the youth and young adult congregation looked to many like a contradiction of it. The "Life-Teen" movement began in Phoenix and subsequently spread across the United States and has migrated to Europe. The theory of this group is to provide music written specifically for teen-aged Catholics, combined with youth ministry to this same group. A Life-Teen Mass would typically take place in the early evening, say at 6:00 p.m., and begin with a half hour of music. There is an insistence that the musicians be quite professional, in the same way that popular youth music is performed by truly excellent musicians. If the youths are accustomed to hearing such secular music as their regular diet, then they must not hear a sub-standard execution of religious music just because it is at Mass.

Another aspect of Life Teen and other youth music is its content. Though youth writers have written specifically liturgical music (e.g., *Mass of a Joyful Heart* by Steve Angrisano and Tom Tomasek, first introduced at the National Catholic Youth Conference in Kansas City, 1997), the main theme of this style of music lies closer to an already existing and very successful protestant movement called Evangelistic or "Christian." In such music, there is conscious use of popular music styles such as Rock, Jamaican, and Gospel, and lyrics that often emphasize personal choice and personal witness.

One of the most successful pieces, "I Will Choose Christ" (1991) by Tom Booth was sung by an artist in the "Christian" recording market and became a hit. The choice of Christ in personal life is of course of great importance to young people, so this piece appeals directly to making sense of life in a troublesome period of time. The lyrics are simple, "I will choose Christ, I will choose love, I choose to serve . . . I give my life to you." The melody also is quite uncomplicated, yet attractive.

Tom Booth's strategy is to confine the majority of the refrain to a three-note interval, ranging from F# to D—except for the last note of each half, which opens the range to a low A (major 6th away). One is reminded again of the strategy for "Ode to Joy." The verses then open out to a wider range, just at the right moment. As with much or most popular music, this limitation of range and chordal structure is balanced by rhythm and forward thrust.

David Haas entered into this field for a few years, but since then has withdrawn from it. In 1999, Oregon Catholic Press published a youth hymnal, *Spirit and Song*, featuring over two hundred pieces in the style or adaptable to it. The editor, Tom Tomasek, paid special attention to how the music fits into the liturgical structure of Mass. Included are Booth, Angrisano, Tomasek, Greg Hayakawa, Ken Canedo, Cyprian Consiglio (the same composer who has now turned to chant and to world music after music in this type), Bobby Fisher, Jesse Manibusan, and borrowings from former popular pieces by such composers as Dan Schutte, Christopher Walker, John Michael Talbot, and Janet Vogt.

The movement has been most successful. As with any approach to popular music for church use, Life Teen has attracted its critics. Teen music seems to exclude those parish and family members who are past this stage of life. Indeed, the congregations for many of these Masses are composed mainly of teen-agers. However, it is not the Church that has made such division between young and old, but the popular music industry, the teen-agers, and commercial interests. If the young people are already captured by their own music, why should the Church not enter in? Moreover, even though the appeal is quite directly to youths, parents often accompany their sons or daughters, establishing family unity instead of the opposite. But critics must be given their due. Their argument is that the family belongs together, and that if the music at a normal Sunday Mass does not please young people, then there is something wrong with the music. It will be of great interest to see which opinion lasts longer: the critics or the teens.

Ethnic Music

Publishers have shown great interest in the emerging fact of Hispanic Roman Catholic churches in the United States. Such composers as Jaime Cortez (*Qué Alegría / I Rejoiced*), Juan Sosa (*Desde la Aurora hasta el Ocaso*), Donna Peña ("Digo 'Sí,' Señor / I Say 'Yes,' Lord"), Pedro Rubalcava (*Deo Gratias*), Rufino Zaragoza (*Misa Juan Diego*), Bob Hurd (*Pan de Vida*), and Mary Francis Reza (*Aclamamos al Señor*) are among the many composers who are contributing Hispanic and bi-lingual music during this period. *Flor Y Canto*, the Spanish-language hymnal published by OCP, is now into its second edition, with over four hundred songs.

Vietnamese music has been helped greatly by Rufino Zaragoza, whose *Longing Heart/Con Tim Khát Khao* is an instrumental collection of Vietnamese melodies, and who served as editor of *Chung Loi Tan Tung/United In Faith And Song: Thanh Ca Song Ngu/Hymns and Songs in Vietnamese and English*, published by OCP.

African American music has been represented from the beginning of the renewal by such composers as the brilliant Clarence Rivers ("God Is Love"), Leon Roberts, Grayson Warren Brown, among others, and of course, by African American Spirituals. This rich repertory is reflected in *Lead Me, Guide Me: The African American Catholic Hymnal* from GIA.

One problem with all ethnic-derived music, of course, is the question of who writes it. If already trained and recognized composers write in the language and style of minority culture, they can easily be seen as intruders into communities not theirs. If they do not, then the talent and success of already popular liturgical music and composers seems denied to important sub-groupings of Catholics. It does look as if new composers will be developing from within American ethnic communities, which will help solidify the identity of the heritage and build upon it.

Hymnbooks and Missalettes abound in this period, far too many to fit within the scope of this chapter. OCP, whose *Today's Missal* yearly publication is the most popular of the worship aids, also puts out a yearly "Music Issue" to supplement the small amount of music that can fit into a missalette. Now the dispute arises as to whether the number of new pieces in this annual music publication makes it worth the price, or whether hymnals, published for example by GIA, are not more economical and give the music in a better form. And so the road goes on.

CONCLUSION

No one can know what lies ahead for liturgical music in the United States. In the over 30 years of experience since Vatican II music has followed a pathway not easy to trace without losing sight of the forest or of the trees or of portions of both. The new version of the *General Instruction of the Roman Missal* (GIRM) has just been promulgated as I write this chapter. As is to be expected, the provisions in this authoritative document include mandates on music and on text for such music. *Liturgiam Authenticam*, released in May, 2001, directs that sung texts and liturgical hymns "should remain relatively fixed so that confusion among the people may be avoided." It further states that, by 2006, the Conferences of Bishops must submit a directory or repertory of texts intended for liturgical singing.[16] The implications of these and other documents will be major for the trajectory of liturgical music in the USA. More than anything else, such propositions will continue to move Masses and other liturgies toward the solemn, the ritual, and a more formal style, away from the communitarian approach we have seen in the first two periods above. Specifically forbidden, for instance, is the use of re-worded psalm songs for the Responsorial. What will this mean for cultural adaptations that use the repertory of psalms provided by GIA in *Gather* hymnal, all of which are popular and few if any of which contain the translation approved by the Congregation For Divine Worship?

Questions such as these are beyond the scope of this present chapter, and have to be subsumed into the too often used phrase, "we shall see." In any case, the hunch of the present writer is that a new period is presently beginning, and that the end of the story has by no means been reached. Ritual transformation continues, sometimes at a dizzying pace, other times like a snail. Perhaps there will yet be time to add Period Four to this talk, as time goes by.

---

[16] *Liturgiam Authenticam*, #108: "Sung texts and liturgical hymns have a particular importance and efficacy. Especially on Sunday, the 'Day of the Lord,' the singing of the faithful gathered for the celebration of Holy Mass, no less than the prayers, the readings and the homily, express in an authentic way the message of the Liturgy while fostering a sense of common faith and communion in charity.

"If they are used widely by the faithful, they should remain relatively fixed so that confusion among the people may be avoided. Within five years from the publication of this Instruction, the Conferences of Bishops, necessarily in collaboration with the national and diocesan Commissions and with other experts, shall provide for the publication of a directory or repertory of texts intended for liturgical singing. This document shall be transmitted for the necessary *recognitio* to the Congregation for Divine Worship and the Discipline of the Sacraments."

John Foley, s.j., Distinguished Liturgical Theologian at Saint Louis University, teaches liturgical and aesthetic theology and is the director of the Center for Liturgy at that same university.